D1364899

Gallery Books
Editor Peter Fallon

ARISTOCRATS

Brian Friel

ARISTOCRATS

Gallery Books

Aristocrats
was first published
by The Gallery Press in 1980.
Reprinted 1983, 1990 and 1999.
Reset 2005.

The Gallery Press
Loughcrew
Oldcastle
County Meath
Ireland

© Brian Friel 1980

ISBN 0 904011 11 9

A CIP catalogue record for this book
is available from the British Library.

The lines quoted in the play are from a poem entitled
'My Father Dying' by Alastair Reid from his book
Weathering (Canongate, Edinburgh). The song 'Sweet
Alice' was written by J Kneass © 1933, Amsco Music
Sales Co, New York.

All rights whatsoever in this play are strictly
reserved. Requests to reproduce the text in whole
or in part should be addressed to the publishers.
Application for performance in any medium should
be addressed to the author's sole agent The Agency
(London) Ltd, (attention Leah Schmidt), 24 Pottery
Lane, Holland Park, London W11 4LZ

for K.H.H.
with affection and gratitude

Aristocrats was first performed in the Abbey Theatre, Dublin, on Thursday, 8 March 1979, with the following cast:

WILLIE DIVER	*Niall O'Brien*
TOM HOFFNUNG	*Kevin McHugh*
UNCLE GEORGE	*Bill Foley*
CASIMIR	*John Kavanagh*
ALICE	*Dearbhla Molloy*
EAMON	*Stephen Rea*
CLAIRE	*Ingrid Craigie*
JUDITH	*Kate Flynn*
FATHER	*Geoff Golden*
ANNA'S VOICE	*Kathleen Barrington*
Direction	*Joe Dowling*
Setting and Costumes	*Wendy Shea*
Lighting	*Leslie Scott*

Time and Place

Summer, mid-1970s. Ballybeg Hall, the home of District Justice O'Donnell, a large and decaying house overlooking the village of Ballybeg, County Donegal, Ireland.

Most of the action takes place outside the south side of the house. Most recently it was a lawn that has not been cared for in years. Before that it was a grass tennis court and before that a croquet lawn — but no trace of these activities remains.

The lawn stretches right across the full front of stage and upstage left (left and right from point of view of audience) where it halts at a tall grey gable with uncurtained windows.

Upstage left is a gazebo, with a pagoda roof and badly weather-beaten. A rusty iron seat inside. The gazebo is made of wood and is about to collapse.

A small room — the study — occupies upstage right. One step up into it from the lawn. And it is separated from the lawn by two invisible walls. On the third wall, parallel to front of stage, is an early Victorian writing desk. The fourth wall, at right angles to front of stage, has a huge marble fireplace. In front of the fireplace is a chaise longue. In the centre of this study a small table, etc, etc, sufficient furnishings to indicate when the hall flourished and to suggest its present decline.

Downstage right a broken sundial mounted on a stone plinth.

Music

All Chopin piano music.

ACT ONE

Scherzo No.2 in B minor, Op.31
Ballade in G minor, Op.23
Waltz in G sharp major, Op.70, No.1
Sonata No.3, Op.58, third movement only: largo
Waltz in E sharp major (Posth)
Waltz in A sharp major (Posth)

ACT TWO

Étude No.3 in E major
Nocturne in F sharp major, Op.15, No.2

ACT THREE

Sonata No.2 in B minor, Op.35, middle section of third movement
Ballade in A flat major, Op.47

ACT ONE

Early afternoon on a very warm summer day.

The opening bars of Scherzo No.2 in B minor fill the study and the lawn, then fade to background.

TOM HOFFNUNG is seated at the table in the study, copying the titles of books into his notebook. He is a quiet, calm, measured American academic in his mid-fifties.

Inside the door leading out to the hall is WILLIE DIVER. He is in his mid-thirties and is from the village. He is standing on a chair and attaching a small speaker to the door frame (he is standing on his jacket to protect the seat of the chair).

Both men work for a few seconds in silence.

Now UNCLE GEORGE enters from the hall. He is in his late seventies; a brother of Father's. Panama hat, walking stick, very old and creased off-white linen suit with an enormous red silk handkerchief spilling out of the breast pocket, trousers stopping well above his ankles. His mouth never stops working, vigorously masticating imaginary food. All his gestures are informed with great energy, as if he were involved in some urgent business.

He is halfway across the study before he realizes that there are other people in the room. Then he stops, stands still, stares at them.

TOM   Hi!

Pause.

WILLIE   Hello, Mister George.
TOM   Come right through. I'm almost finished here.

GEORGE hesitates — then turns and exits through the door.

That's the third time he's attempted to come in here.

	Maybe I should go somewhere else.
WILLIE	Not at all. He dodges about like that all the time.
TOM	Does he never speak?
WILLIE	They say he does. I never heard him.
TOM	And he's a brother of the District Justice — is that correct?
WILLIE	That's it. Fierce man for the booze when he was only a young fellow — drunk himself half crazy. Then all of a sudden packed it in. And stopped speaking.
TOM	I wonder why.
WILLIE	They say about here that when he wasn't going to be asking for drink, he thought it wasn't worth saying anything. But brains — d'you see Mister George? — the smartest of the whole connection, they say.

He gets down from the chair, removes his jacket, carefully rubs the seat with his sleeve.

	Could you give us a second, Tom?
TOM	How's it going?
WILLIE	Nearly finished now.

TOM *joins him at the door.*

TOM	Judith's really going to be pleased with this.
WILLIE	Do you think so?
TOM	Sure she will. What can I do?
WILLIE	Show her this when she comes down, will you? There's a volume control at the side here — loud or soft, whatever way she wants it.
TOM	Right.
WILLIE	And if she wants to turn it off altogether, there's a switch at the bottom here — d'you see?
TOM	Got it.
WILLIE	I haven't put it up too high for her, have I? What d'you think?
TOM	Looks about right to me.
WILLIE	An ugly-looking aul' yoke in a room like this, isn't it?

TOM	You wouldn't notice it. It's a good job, Willie.
WILLIE	Indeed and it's rough enough. But it'll save her running up and down them stairs every turnabout.
TOM	Is it on now?
WILLIE	I've still to connect it to the lead from the bedroom. Hold on a minute.

> WILLIE *goes out to the hall.* TOM *returns to the table. Just before he sits down,* CASIMIR *enters left, carrying deckchairs.* CASIMIR *is the only son of the house; in his thirties. Despite the heat he is wearing a knitted V-neck pullover under his sports jacket. One immediately gets a sense that there is something different about him — as he says himself, 'peculiar'. But what it is is elusive: partly his shyness, partly his physical movements, particularly the way he walks — rapid, jerky, without ease or grace — partly his erratic enthusiasm, partly his habit of suddenly grinning and giving a mirthless 'ha-ha' at unlikely times, usually when he is distressed. But he is not a buffoon nor is he 'disturbed'. He is a perfectly normal man with distinctive and perhaps slightly exaggerated mannerisms. He now stands at the step just outside the study and talks to* TOM.

CASIMIR	Claire.
TOM	Yeah.
CASIMIR	Playing the piano.
TOM	Sure.
CASIMIR	My sister Claire.
TOM	I know.
CASIMIR	Welcome home recital for me.
TOM	Some welcome.
CASIMIR	Dexterity — simplicity — passion — Claire has everything.
TOM	She certainly —

> *But* CASIMIR *has gone and now stands in the middle of the lawn.*

CASIMIR   Claire!
CLAIRE   Yes?
CASIMIR   Play the G minor ballade.

The music stops.

CLAIRE   Which?
CASIMIR   The G minor.
CLAIRE   I'm not in the mood for that, Casimir.
CASIMIR   Special request. Please.
CLAIRE   Just a bit of it, then.

> *He stands listening. She begins in the middle of the G minor ballade, Op.23, just immediately before the molto crescendo, after three bars.*

CASIMIR   Yes-yes-yes-yes-yes!

> *He sings a few bars with the piano, conducting at the same time — he is radiant with delight. Then he returns to the step.*

The G minor. Wonderful, isn't it?
TOM   Yeah.

> CASIMIR *sings a few more bars.*

CASIMIR   When I think of Ballybeg Hall it's always like this: the sun shining; the doors and windows all open; the place filled with music.

> *He is suddenly off again — left — for more deck-chairs. The sound of static from the speaker. Then* FATHER's *laboured breathing.* TOM *listens.*

JUDITH   That's the best lunch you've had in days. Let me wipe your chin.

> FATHER's *incoherent mumbling.*

It's very warm. I don't think you need this quilt, do
you?

Incoherent mumbling. TOM *goes to the speaker.*
He stands listening.

Oh, Father, you've soiled your pyjamas again! Why
didn't you tell me?

FATHER   Judith?
JUDITH   Come on. Let's get them changed.
FATHER   Where's Judith?
JUDITH   I'm Judith.
FATHER   Where's Judith?
JUDITH   I'm here beside you, Father.
FATHER   Where's Claire?
JUDITH   In the drawing room.
FATHER   Where's Claire?
JUDITH   Can't you hear her? She's playing the piano for you.
          Lift your leg, Father.
FATHER   Where's Alice?
JUDITH   Everybody's here.
FATHER   Where's Casimir?
JUDITH   Everybody's at home. They're all downstairs.
FATHER   Where's Anna?
JUDITH   Anna's in Africa — you know that. Now — the other
          leg. Father, please, I can't get them off unless you
          help me.
FATHER   Where's Judith? Where's Claire? Where's Casimir?
          Where's Alice? Where's —
JUDITH   They're all here. They're all downstairs.
FATHER   Let me tell you something in confidence: Judith
          betrayed the family.
JUDITH   Did she?
FATHER   I don't want to make an issue of it. But I can tell you
          confidentially — Judith betrayed us.
JUDITH   That's better. Now you're more comfortable.
FATHER   Great betrayal; enormous betrayal.
JUDITH   Let me feel those tops. Are they wet, too?
FATHER   But Anna's praying for her. Did you know that?

JUDITH	Yes, I know, Father.
FATHER	Anna has the whole convent praying for her.
JUDITH	Now let's get these clean ones on. Lift this leg again.
FATHER	Where's Judith? Where's Alice? Where's Casimir? Where's Claire?

WILLIE *returns, carrying a parcel of two bottles of whiskey.* TOM *pretends to consult his notebook.*

WILLIE	That's her hooked up. Any sound out of her?
TOM	Yeah; something was said a moment ago. Seems to be working fine.

WILLIE *examines the speaker.*

WILLIE	Aye, it should be. She'd need to have this whole house rewired — half of them fittings is dangerous.
TOM	Is she aware of that?
WILLIE	Sure it would cost her a fortune. Tell her I'll take a run in later and sink them bare wires. And I'll leave this (*parcel*) here for her. A drop of whiskey. I thought maybe, you know, with the family back home and all, she might be a bit short. They come last night, didn't they?
TOM	And a late night it was, too. This'll be very welcome. You'll be going to the wedding, won't you?
WILLIE	Me? Oh damn the fear.
TOM	Will you not?
WILLIE	Not at all; that'll be a family affair. What about yourself?
TOM	I leave tomorrow.
WILLIE	They'll manage without us. (*Leaving*) Well —
TOM	Okay, Willie. You'll be back later?
WILLIE	Aye, sometime. And tell her, too — them groceries she wanted — I left them in the pantry.
TOM	I'll tell her.

FATHER'*s voice suddenly very loud and very authoritative.*

FATHER   Are you proposing that my time and the time of this
          court be squandered while the accused goes home
          and searches for this title which he claims he has in
          a tin box somewhere?

          WILLIE *is startled and delighted.*

WILLIE   Himself by Jaysus!
JUDITH   Now this leg — that's it — that's great.
FATHER   And that we sit in this freezing court until he comes
          back? Is that what you propose, Sergeant?
JUDITH   Raise your body just a little.
FATHER   Because I can tell you I won't have it — I will not
          have it!
WILLIE   Himself by Jaysus, guldering away!
JUDITH   That's more comfortable.
FATHER   We're all petrified in this place as it is — really
          petrified. And I will not endure it a second longer.
          Case dismissed. Court adjourned.
JUDITH   Now over on your side and I'll tuck you in and
          you'll sleep for a while.

          A few short mumbling sounds from FATHER; *then
          silence.*

WILLIE   D'you hear that for a voice, eh? By Jaysus, isn't he a
          powerful fighting aul' man all the time, eh?
TOM   Would you believe it! I've been here four days and
          I've never seen him yet.
WILLIE   Sure he hasn't been down the stairs since the stroke
          felled him. But before that — haul' your tongue, man
          — oh be Jaysus he was a sight to behold — oh be
          Jaysus!

          CASIMIR *has entered left with more deckchairs
          which he sets up on the lawn. He now enters the study.*

CASIMIR   Always Chopin — the great love of her life. She
          could play all the nocturnes and all the waltzes before

17

	she was ten. We thought we had a little Mozart on our hands. And on her sixteenth birthday she got a scholarship to go to Paris. But Father — you've met Father?
TOM	Actually I —
CASIMIR	'An itinerant musician? (*Wagging finger*) Ho-ho-ho-ho-ho.' Wasn't that naughty of him? (*Sees* WILLIE) Ah!

There is a brief, awkward pause — WILLIE *smiling, expecting to be recognized,* CASIMIR *staring blankly.* WILLIE *finally approaches gauchely.*

WILLIE	How are you, Casimir?
CASIMIR	Yes? Yes? Who have we here?
WILLIE	No, you wouldn't remember me.
CASIMIR	Should I? Should I? Yes, of course I should.
WILLIE	It's —
CASIMIR	Don't — don't tell me — let me guess. I have it — it's Deegan, the jarvey! Am I right?
WILLIE	Jackie Deegan.
CASIMIR	There you are!
WILLIE	Deegan, the car-man; that's right; he's dead; I'm Diver.
CASIMIR	Diver?
WILLIE	From the back shore.
CASIMIR	Ah.
WILLIE	Willie Diver.
CASIMIR	Ah.
WILLIE	Tony Diver's son — the Slooghter Divers. I used to be about the gate lodge when my Uncle Johnny was in it. (*Pause*) Johnny MacLoone and my Auntie Sarah. (*Pause*) That's going back a fair few years now. My Uncle Johnny's dead, too — Jaysus he must be dead thirty years now. (*Pause*) I seen you this morning from the upper hill — I've the land all took from Judith.
TOM	And Willie's just rigged up this thing so that your father can be heard down here now.
CASIMIR	What's that?

TOM   A baby-alarm. Won't that be a help?
CASIMIR   Ah yes; splendid, splendid.
TOM   Save Judith running up and down the stairs.
CASIMIR   Of course; indeed; wonderful; splendid; great idea.
WILLIE   I mind one day Casimir and me — we were only
          cubs this size at the time — the pair of us got into a
          punt down at the slip and cast off — d'you mind? —
          and be Jaysus didn't the tide carry us out.
CASIMIR   Good Lord! Were we drowned?
WILLIE   Damn the bit of us: the wind carried us back in
          again. Nobody knew a damn thing about us except
          ourselves.
CASIMIR   Well, wasn't that wonderful. Ha-ha. (*Suddenly shakes
          Willie's hand*) Marvellous to see you again. It's so
          good to be back again. Do you know how long it's
          been since I was home last? — Eleven years. Now, if
          you'll pardon me — I'm the chef for today!
WILLIE   Surely to God, Casimir.

          CASIMIR *is off again — this time to the gazebo
          where he finds a few more faded seats which he
          carries out to the lawn.*

          Same aul' Casimir.
TOM   Is he?
WILLIE   When he'd come home on holidays from the board-
          ing school, sometimes he'd walk down the village
          street, and we'd all walk in a line behind him, acting
          the maggot, you know, imitating him. And by Jaysus
          he never thought of looking round.
TOM   That expression — you've taken the land from
          Judith — what does it mean?
WILLIE   She has nobody to work it so she lets it out every
          year.
TOM   How many acres are there?
WILLIE   I could hardly tell you. It's all hill and bog.
TOM   So you lease it?
WILLIE   I sort of take it off her hands — you know.
TOM   And you till it?

19

WILLIE	I footer about. I'm no farmer.
TOM	But it's profitable land?
WILLIE	Profitable? (*Laughs*) If you've a pair of wellingtons, we'll walk it some day.

He goes off towards hall. CASIMIR *is arranging the seats into a wide arc. The music suddenly stops.*

CLAIRE	Casimir!

CASIMIR *stops working.*

CASIMIR	Hello-hello.
CLAIRE	Where are you?
CASIMIR	On the tennis court — just beside the tent.
CLAIRE	Can you hear me?
CASIMIR	Clearly.
CLAIRE	I've a test for you: what's the name of this?

CASIMIR *is suddenly excited, suddenly delighted. He rushes to the step.*

CASIMIR	A test! She's testing me! A game we played all the time when we were children!
CLAIRE	Casimir!

He runs back to the centre of the lawn.

CASIMIR	Go ahead! I'm ready! I'm waiting!

He stands poised, waiting. His eyes are shut tight. His fists clenched on his chest. To himself, as he waits in suspense

Ha-ha. Good Lord — good Lord — good Lord — good Lord — good Lord —

The music begins: Waltz in G sharp major, Op.70, No.1.

Oh-oh-oh-it's-it's-it's — (*to himself*) — the McCormack Waltz! (*Clapping his hands in relief and delight and now shouting*) The McCormack Waltz! Right, Claire? Full marks? Amn't I right?

CLAIRE   Can't hear you.

CASIMIR   You can hear me very well. That's it. I know. I *know*.

He runs into the study.

Got it! The McCormack Waltz! It's the G sharp major actually but we call it the McCormack because one night John McCormack, Count John McCormack, you know who I'm talking about? — the tenor? — of course you do! — well, Father had something to do with McCormack getting the papal knighthood — some French cardinal Father knew in the Vatican — and because of that Father and McCormack became great friends.

TOM *begins writing in his notebook.*

TOM   Casimir, this is precisely the material I — may I jot down? —

But CASIMIR *is now back at the door and clapping his hands.*

CASIMIR   Bravo, Claire darling! Bravo, bravo, bravo!

Now he is back into the centre of the room again.

Anyhow McCormack was staying here one night and Mother was in one of her down periods and my goodness when she was like that — oh, my goodness, poor Mother, for weeks on end how unhappy she'd be.

TOM   She was forty-seven when she died?

CASIMIR   Forty-six.

TOM   Had she been ill for long? Was it sudden?

Pause.

CASIMIR   Anyhow, this night Claire played that waltz, the G
           sharp major, and McCormack asked Mother to dance
           and she refused but he insisted, he insisted, and
           finally he got her to the middle of the floor and he
           put his arm around her and then she began to laugh
           and he danced her up and down the hall and then
           in here and then out to the tennis court and you
           could hear their laughing over the whole house and
           finally the pair of them collapsed in the gazebo out
           there. Yes — marvellous! The McCormack Waltz!

TOM   Approximately what year was —

CASIMIR   A great big heavy man — oh, yes, I remember
           McCormack — I remember his enormous jowls
           trembling — but Mother said he danced like Nijinsky.
           (*Suddenly aware*) I'm disturbing your studies, amn't I?

TOM   Actually you're —

CASIMIR   Of course I am. Give me five minutes to make a call
           and then I'll leave you absolutely in peace.

           *As he goes to the phone (an old style phone, with a
           handle at the side) below the fireplace, he picks up
           a cassette player from the mantelpiece.*

           Do you know what I did last night even before I
           unpacked? I made two secret tapes of her to bring
           back to Helga and the children, just to prove to them
           how splendid a pianist she really is.

TOM   Have they never been to Ireland?

           Momentary pause.

CASIMIR   And I'm going to play them this afternoon while
           we're having the picnic. And I've another little
           surprise up my sleeve too: *after* we've eaten. I've got
           a tape that Anna sent me last Christmas!

TOM   Very nice.

CASIMIR   A really tremendous person, Anna. Actually her

name in religion is Sister John Henry and she chose that name because John Henry Newman — you know? — the cardinal? — Cardinal Newman? — of course you do — well, he married Grandfather and Grandmother O'Donnell — in this very room as a matter of fact — special dispensation from Rome. But of course we think of her as Anna. And the tape she sent me has a message for every member of the family. And it'll be so appropriate now that we're all gathered together again.

As he is saying the last few words he is also turning the handle on the phone.

FATHER Don't touch that!

CASIMIR drops the phone in panic and terror.

CASIMIR Christ! Ha-ha. Oh my God! That — that — that's —
TOM It's only the baby-alarm.
CASIMIR I thought for a moment Father was — was — was —
TOM Maybe I should turn it down a bit.
CASIMIR God, it's eerie — that's what it is — eerie — eerie —

The phone suddenly rings — and his panic is revived. He grabs it.

Hello? Hello? Hello? Yes, I did ring, Mrs Moore. I'm sorry, I'm sorry, I'm very sorry. Could you try that call to Germany for me again? The number is Hamburg — Sorry, sorry, yes of course I gave it to you already; I am sorry — Yes, I'll hold on — (*To* TOM *who is watching him*) Helga, my wife — my wife Helga — to let her know I've arrived safely — she worries herself sick if I don't — Yes, just for the wedding on Thursday, to give Claire away, and then straight off again. Yes, indeed I'll tell her that, Mrs Moore. Thank you, thank you. (*To* TOM) Was always terrified of her, absolutely terrified; postmistress in Ballybeg ever since — Yes, yes, I'll hold on.

    TOM *fingers the limp servant's bell beside the fireplace.*

TOM   When did they go out of action?
CASIMIR   What's that?
TOM   The bells.
CASIMIR   Oh I suppose when there was nobody to ring them. Or nobody to obey them. She ought to be at home now.

    CLAIRE *begins playing another nocturne.* ALICE *enters. In her mid-thirties. She is hung-over after last night. As she enters she touches her cheek which has a bruise mark on it.*

ALICE   Morning, everybody.
TOM   It's afternoon, Alice.
ALICE   Is it?

    She blows a kiss to CASIMIR. *He blows one back.*

    Am I the last down?
TOM   Just about. Is Eamon still asleep?
ALICE   He was up and about hours ago. He's gone down to the village to visit his grandmother.
TOM   And how are you today?
ALICE   I misbehaved very badly last night, did I?
TOM   Not at all. You just sat there by yourself, singing nursery rhymes.
ALICE   That's alright. Tom, isn't it?
TOM   Correct.
ALICE   Dr Thomas Hoffnung from Chicago.
TOM   You see — you were in great shape.
CASIMIR   Hoffnung's the German word for hope. So your name's really Tom Hope. Terrific name, Alice, isn't it? — Tom Hope! Calling Hamburg.

ALICE   What?

CASIMIR   Helga.

ALICE   Give her my love.

CASIMIR   She's in terrific form today.

ALICE   Is she?

CASIMIR   Claire.

ALICE   Oh — yes, yes. (*She shades her eyes with her hand and looks outside*) Is it cold?

TOM   No, it's a beautiful day.

She sits on the step and holds her head in her hands. TOM *moves back to* CASIMIR *who is anchored by the phone.*

Perhaps you could confirm a few facts for me, Casimir. This is where Gerard Manley Hopkins used to sit — is that correct?

CASIMIR   Look at the armrest and you'll see a stain on it.

TOM   Where?

CASIMIR   The other arm — at the front.

TOM   Got it.

CASIMIR   He used to recite 'The Wreck of the *Deutschland*' to Grandmother O'Donnell and he always rested his teacup just there; and one afternoon he knocked it over and burned his right hand very severely.

TOM *is writing all this information down.*

TOM   That would have been about — ?

CASIMIR   Shhh. Yes, Mrs Moore? Sorry, sorry? Yes-yes-yes — of course — thank you — thank you. (*He hangs up*) Something wrong with the lines. Can't even get the Letterkenny exchange. Poor old Helga'll think I've deserted her. Tell me again, Tom — I'm ashamed to say I've forgotten — what's the title of you research?

TOM   I can hardly remember it myself.

CASIMIR   No, no, please, please.

TOM   'Recurring cultural, political and social modes in the upper strata of Roman Catholic society in rural

	Ireland since the act of Catholic Emancipation.'
CASIMIR	Good heavens. Ha-ha.
TOM	I know. It's awful. I apologise.
CASIMIR	No, no, no, don't apologise. It sounds very — it sounds — Alice, isn't it very, very? — Right, let's be systematic. Judith has shown you the family records and the old estate papers, hasn't she?
TOM	Yeah.
CASIMIR	And you've seen all the old diaries in the library?
TOM	That's all covered.
CASIMIR	Splendid, splendid. So what you want now is — well, what?
TOM	Family lore, family reminiscences. For example, where did this (*crucifix*) come from?
CASIMIR	Cardinal O'Donnell; present from Salamanca. No relation, just a great family friend. And a Donegal man, of course; a neighbour, almost. Remember him, Alice?
ALICE	Who?
CASIMIR	Cardinal O'Donnell.
ALICE	Do I remember him? He must be dead seventy years.
CASIMIR	He's not.
ALICE	At least.
CASIMIR	Is he? Ah. Good heavens. I suppose you're right. In that case. Well, let's see what else we have. Oh, yes, everything has some association. Hopkins you know.

TOM *begins writing.*

TOM	Got that.
CASIMIR	And this is Chesterton.
TOM	Sorry?
CASIMIR	G K Chesterton.
TOM	The ashtray?
CASIMIR	The footstool.
TOM	Foot- —
CASIMIR	He was giving an imitation of Lloyd George making a speech and he lost his balance and — Kraask! — Bam! — Smaak! — Boom! — down on his back across

| | the fender. And you know the weight of Chesterton — he must be twenty stone! The fender's still dented, isn't it, Alice? |
| ALICE | Yes. |

She goes out to the lawn and sits on one of the deckchairs. CLAIRE *begins to play Sonata No.3, Op.58, third movement.*

CASIMIR	Sprained elbow and bruised ribs.
TOM	Great.
CASIMIR	Laid up in the nursery for five days.
TOM	That could have been when? — doesn't matter — I'll check it out. How often did he visit Ballybeg Hall?
CASIMIR	Oh, I've no idea — often, often, often — oh, yes. And Father and Mother spent part of their honeymoon with him in England, (*to* ALICE) didn't they? — (*Sees she is gone*) Oh, they were very close friends. Father wanted me to be christened Gilbert Keith but Mother insisted on Casimir — he was a Polish prince — Mother liked that. And this (*chaise longue*) is Daniel O'Connell, the Liberator — tremendous horseman, O'Connell — see the mark of his riding-boots? And that's the 58 —
TOM	The clock?
CASIMIR	Chopin sonata — third movement.
TOM	Oh.
CASIMIR	And this (*candlestick*) is George Moore, the writer — I wonder why that's George Moore — I've no idea — I just know it's George Moore. And this (*book*) is Tom Moore — you know — Byron's friend — (*sings*) 'Believe me if all those endearing young charms/ which I gaze on so fondly today.' And this (*Bible*) is Hilaire Belloc; wedding present to Father and Mother. And this is Yeats. And —
TOM	What's Yeats?
CASIMIR	This cushion (*on chaise longue*).
TOM	Cushion — Yeats —
CASIMIR	Oh, he was — he was just tremendous, Yeats, with

27

CASIMIR | those cold, cold eyes of his. Oh, yes, I remember Yeats vividly.
TOM | That would have been when you were — ?
CASIMIR | On one occasion sat up three nights in succession, just there, on Daniel O'Connell, with his head on that cushion and his feet on Chesterton, just because someone had told him we were haunted. Can you imagine! Three full nights! But of course we weren't haunted. There was never a ghost in the Hall. Father wouldn't believe in ghosts. And he was quite peeved about it; oh, quite peeved. 'You betrayed me, Bernard,' he said to Father. 'You betrayed me,' and those cold eyes of his burning with —

He breaks off suddenly because CLAIRE *has switched from the sonata to a waltz — E sharp major (Posth) — 'The Bedtime Waltz'.*

Listen! Listen! The Bedtime Waltz! Oh, that's my favourite — that's easily my favourite.

He joins ALICE *outside.*

Alice, do you know what that is?
ALICE | (*sings*) 'Now off to bed, my darlings,
It's time to say goodnight'

CASIMIR *and* ALICE *sing together.*

'So up the stairs, my sweethearts,
And soon you'll be sleeping tight.'

TOM *has joined them outside.*

CASIMIR | Beautiful, isn't it? Oh, that's easily my favourite; oh, easily, easily. The Bedtime Waltz. It's the E sharp major actually but we call it the Bedtime — don't we, Alice? — because as soon as Mother'd begin to play it, we'd have to dash upstairs — remember? —

dash upstairs and wash ourselves and say our night prayers and be in bed before she'd finished. Isn't it so beautiful? (*Sings*) 'Now off to bed, my darlings . . .'

They all listen to the music for a few moments.

My God, isn't she playing well? The impending marriage — that's what it is: the concentration of delight and fear and expectation. And Judith tells me she's been in really bubbling humour for months and months — not one day of depression. Not even one; maybe she's grown out of it. Isn't it marvellous? May I tell you something, Tom? We always said among ourselves, Judith and Alice and I, isn't this true, Alice?

ALICE   Isn't what true?

CASIMIR   We always said — well, no, it was never quite expressed; but we always, you know, we always suspected — amn't I right, Alice?

ALICE   What are you saying, Casimir?

CASIMIR   Just that we always thought that perhaps Claire darling was the type of girl, you know, the kind of girl — we always had the idea that our little Claire was one of those highly sensitive, highly intelligent young girls who might choose — who might elect to remain single in life. Ha-ha. That's what we thought. Isn't that true, Alice?

ALICE   And we were wrong.

CASIMIR   Indeed we were wrong! Thank goodness we were wrong! Not that she isn't an attractive girl, a *very* attractive girl — isn't she attractive, Tom? — don't you find Claire attractive?

ALICE   For God's sake, Casimir —

CASIMIR   What's wrong with that? Tom finds little Claire attractive or he doesn't find her attractive?

TOM   She's a very personable young lady.

CASIMIR   Personable — that's the word — an excellent word — personable. Of course she is. And such a sweet

	nature. And her young man, I gather, is an excep-tionally fine type. You've met him, Tom, have you?
TOM	Just once — briefly.
CASIMIR	I'm really looking forward to meeting him. Aren't you, Alice? A mature man who neither smokes nor drinks and —
ALICE	A middle-aged widower with four young children.
CASIMIR	That's fine — that's fine. Claire is exceptionally good with children. Judith told me that when she was giving those piano lessons to the children in the village —
ALICE	What lessons? What children?
CASIMIR	All last winter she went every evening to five or six houses until — you know — poor old Claire — the old trouble — over-anxiety, that's all it is basically, I'm sure that's all it is — and when she had to give it up, I'm sure she missed the pin-money — I mean she must have — what was I talking about? Yes, all those children. Judith wrote and told me they were devoted to her — Judith told me that. And her young man, Jerry, runs a very successful green-grocer's business and he has a great white lorry with an enormous plastic banana on top of the cab and he supplies wonderful fresh vegetables to all the hotels within a twenty-mile radius and he's also an accomplished trumpet player and they play duets together. Good. Good. It all sounds just — just — just so splendid and so — so appropriate. Everything's in hand. Everything's under control. I'm so happy, so happy for her. Ha-ha.

His head rotates between ALICE *and* TOM *in very rapid movements, staring at them with his fixed, anguished smile. Silence. Then suddenly the music changes — a waltz — A sharp major (Posth).*

	Dance with me, Alice.
ALICE	Casimir.
CASIMIR	(*Shouts*) Clever, clever, Claire! Bravo! (*To* ALICE) Please.

ALICE	Not now.
CASIMIR	In celebration.
ALICE	You never could dance.
CASIMIR	Try me — come on — come on!
ALICE	Please. I'm —

He grabs her hand and pulls her to her feet.

CASIMIR	One-two-three One-two-three —
ALICE	For God's sake —
CASIMIR	One-two-three One-two-three —
ALICE	Casimir!
CASIMIR	(*Sings*) Alice and Casimir Alice and Casimir Alice and Casimir One-two-three One-two-three —

He is now dancing with the reluctant ALICE *and singing so loudly that he does not hear the phone ring.*

TOM	Your call, Casimir!
CASIMIR	Over and round again Back and forth, down again —
TOM	Casimir!
CASIMIR	Isn't she terrific! And an even better ballet dancer, and she has certificates in French to prove it!
TOM	Call to Hamburg!
CASIMIR	What?
TOM	Germany!

CASIMIR *stops suddenly. He hears the phone now. The high spirits vanish instantly.*

CASIMIR	God — Helga — that'll be Helga! Ha-ha.

He runs into the study and grabs the phone.

Halloh? Halloh? Helga? Bist du da, Helga? Halloh?
Halloh?

ALICE *flops into a seat.*

TOM   I'm sorry I can't dance.
ALICE   Thank God for that. Is that whiskey I saw in there?
TOM   Can I get you some?
ALICE   Would you, please?

TOM *goes into the study and picks up the drinks
tray.*

CASIMIR   Yes, yes, I'm holding, Mrs Moore, I'm holding. (*To*
TOM) Terrific!
TOM   You're through?
CASIMIR   Yes.
TOM   Good.
CASIMIR   To Letterkenny. (*Into phone*) Very well, thank you,
Mrs Moore — they're all very well. And how is Mr
Moore keeping? Oh, good Lord, I never heard that
— Six years ago? Oh, good heavens, I'm very sorry
— (*To* TOM) Ha-ha.

TOM *carries the tray outside.*

ALICE   Has he got through?
TOM   I think not quite.
ALICE   Sometimes when I ring home from London it takes
me two hours.
TOM   Hey, you've hurt your cheek.
ALICE   Have I? Must have bumped into something last
night. It's not sore. Have a drink yourself.
TOM   I will, thanks. Do you come home often?
ALICE   You're not going to interrogate me again, are you?
TOM   Would you mind?
ALICE   I don't know any answers.
TOM   When you were growing up, did you mix at all with
the local people?

32

ALICE   We're 'local people'.

TOM   Sure; but you're gentry; you're big house.

ALICE   Eamon's local — Eamon's from the village.

TOM   But as kids did you play with other Ballybeg kids?

ALICE   We were sent off to boarding school when we were seven or eight.

TOM   Casimir, too?

ALICE   He went to the Benedictines when he was six.

TOM   Wow. And afterwards?

ALICE   After we left boarding school? Judith and Claire and I went to a convent in Carcassonne — a finishing school — and became — young ladies, (*raises glass*) didn't we?

TOM   Indeed. And Casimir?

ALICE   Began Law in the family tradition but always hated books. So he left home — went to England — worked at various 'genteel' jobs. Then he met Helga and she took him off to Germany. I think he works part-time in a food-processing factory — I don't want to ask him. Helga's the real breadwinner: she's a cashier in a bowling alley. Anything else?

TOM   Tell me about Eamon.

She rises and fills her glass again.

ALICE   Didn't we talk about that last night?

TOM   Briefly.

ALICE   What did I tell you?

He consults his notebook.

TOM   'Poised for a brilliant career in the diplomatic service when — '

ALICE   'Poised for a — ' I never said that!

TOM   I'm quoting you.

ALICE   I *must* have been drunk.

TOM   Then the Civil Rights movement began in the North in '68. The Dublin government sent him to Belfast as an observer and after a few months of observing and

	reporting he joined the movement. Was sacked, of course. Moved to England and is now a probation officer with the Greater London Council. Right?
ALICE	Listen — Claire's tired at last.
TOM	What was your father's attitude?
ALICE	To Eamon?
TOM	To the Civil Rights campaign.
ALICE	He opposed it. No, that's not accurate. He was indifferent: that was across the Border — away in the North.
TOM	Only twenty miles away.
ALICE	Politics never interested him. Politics are vulgar.
TOM	And Judith? What was her attitude? Was she engaged?
ALICE	She took part in the Battle of the Bogside. Left Father and Uncle George and Claire alone here and joined the people in the streets fighting the police. That's an attitude, isn't it? That's when Father had his first stroke. And seven months later she had a baby by a Dutch reporter. Does that constitute sufficient engagement?

They are interrupted by the sound of laughter and horseplay from the hall.

CLAIRE	Give me that, Eamon!
EAMON	Jump for it!
CLAIRE	I'm warning you!
CASIMIR	Shhhhh — please!
EAMON	Jump-jump-jump-jump-jump!
CLAIRE	Eamon, I'm telling you!
EAMON	Doesn't it suit me?

They burst into the study — EAMON wearing the headdress of Claire's wedding outfit. She is trying to recover it. EAMON is in his thirties. CLAIRE, the youngest daughter, is in her twenties. At this moment she is in one of her high moods: talkative, playful, energetic. On other occasions she is solitary and silent and withdrawn. They are now in the study.

34

CLAIRE	Beautiful on you. Now give it back to me at once!
CASIMIR	Please — please.
EAMON	Sorry.
CASIMIR	Hamburg.
EAMON	What?
CASIMIR	Helga.
EAMON	Ah. (*To* CLAIRE) Behave yourself.
CASIMIR	Looking marvellous.
EAMON	Me?
CASIMIR	Splendid.
EAMON	Hung-over.
CASIMIR	You weren't drunk.
CLAIRE	He was full.
EAMON	Great cure this morning.
CASIMIR	The E sharp major, Claire? The Bedtime — wasn't I right?
CLAIRE	Full marks.

EAMON *suddenly stoops down to the level of the mouthpiece of the phone and speaks rapidly into it.*

EAMON	'Mrs Moore isn't poor — '
CASIMIR	Eamon — !
EAMON	'Mrs Moore's a rich aul' hoor!'
CASIMIR	Oh, God!
CLAIRE	Troublemaker! Come on!
EAMON	See you outside, Casimir.
CASIMIR	No, nothing, Mrs Moore — I didn't speak — sorry — sorry —

CLAIRE *has* EAMON *by the arm and drags him outside. As he goes he bumps into the chaise longue, the table, etc. As he does*

EAMON	Begging your pardon, your eminence, your worship, your holiness — sorry, Shakespeare, Lenin, Mickey Mouse, Marilyn Monroe —

They are now out on the lawn.

35

Like walking through Madame Tussaud's, isn't it, Professor? Or a bloody minefield?

CLAIRE *grabs her headdress from his head.*

CLAIRE	Thank you.
EAMON	Won't she be a beautiful bride?
TOM	Certainly will.
CLAIRE	Lucky for you it's not soiled.
ALICE	Let's see it, Claire.
CLAIRE	I'm going to shorten that net.
ALICE	Very smart. Did you get it in Derry?
CLAIRE	Judith made it. And the dress. And her own outfit, too. Economy.
ALICE	It's very pretty.
CLAIRE	Did you know that on the morning Grandmother O'Donnell got married the whole village was covered with bunting and she gave a gold sovereign to every child under twelve? And the morning Mother got married she distributed roses to everyone in the chapel. I was wondering what I could do — what about a plastic bag of vegetables to every old-age pensioner? I suppose it'll soon be lunchtime, won't it?
TOM	That was great music. (*She looks directly at him and does not speak. He feels he has to add something*) Really wonderful. I enjoyed it. Really great.
CLAIRE	No, it wasn't.
TOM	I thought it was.
CLAIRE	I'm only a good pianist. I'm not a great pianist. I thought I was once. But I know I'm not.
EAMON	(*To* TOM) So there!
ALICE	Is this what you're going to shorten?
CLAIRE	Maybe. I don't know. What do you think?
ALICE	Let's see it on.
EAMON	(*To* ALICE) Granny sends her warmest love. (ALICE *turns away from him*) She was disappointed you weren't with me but I said you had a headache. That wasn't a lie, was it?

ALICE *ignores him. She addresses* CLAIRE.

ALICE   Maybe a fraction of an inch; but I like it as it is.

EAMON   Down in the village visiting my grandmother, Professor.

TOM   So I understand.

EAMON   Reared me from a pup, you might say. When I was three, the family had to emigrate to Scotland for work and I was left behind with Granny. (*Arms around* CLAIRE) Her very special love to you, she says. And she's sending up a small present tomorrow.

CLAIRE I called in with her the day before yesterday.

EAMON   And brought her yellow roses.

CLAIRE But I can't persuade her to come to the wedding.

EAMON   All she wanted is to be asked. And you were wearing a white cotton dress and a pale blue headscarf and you looked like an angel. (*He hugs her briefly and releases her*) Over the years, Professor, I've lusted after each of the three O'Donnell girls in turn. (*Sees the drink*) Where was this hidden? I thought we guzzled every drop of booze in the house last night?

TOM   Willie brought it.

EAMON   Willie who?

CLAIRE Willie who!

TOM   Willie Diver.

EAMON   Of course. Willie Slooghter, the ardent suitor. Sorry I missed him.

TOM   He'll be back later. He was putting up the baby-alarm for Judith. See — on the door frame.

CLAIRE That's going to be a great help.

EAMON *raises his glass to the speaker.*

EAMON   The judicial presence restored. District Justice O'Donnell, Sir, welcome downstairs again. (*To* CLAIRE) Is it true that Willie practically haunts the place?

CLAIRE A little bit, I'm afraid. But he's very helpful to Judith; and very generous.

37

CLAIRE *now sits and begins to sew her headdress.*
ALICE *drifts upstage and sits alone in the gazebo.*
TOM *sits close to the sundial and glances through his notes.*

EAMON   Always was. One civil and one decent man. (*Drinks*) Your good health, William. D'you know what someone in the pub was telling me this morning? He has five hundred slot-machines in amusement arcades all round the county. Can you imagine? He'd be worth a fortune if he looked after them but he never goes near them! I'm sorry — Claire? (*Offering a drink*)

CLAIRE   The doctor doesn't allow me to take alcohol when I'm on sedatives.

EAMON   Aren't you a wise and obedient girl. Professor?

TOM   It's Tom. I'm okay.

EAMON   That's someone you should meet.

TOM   Who's that?

EAMON   My grandmother. You'd find her interesting. Worked all her life as a maid here in the Hall.

TOM   In the Hall? Here?

EAMON   Didn't you know that? Oh, yes, yes. Something like fifty-seven years continuous service with the District Justice and his wife, Lord have mercy on her; and away back to the earlier generation, with his father, the High Court Judge, and his family. Oh, you should meet her before you leave — a fund of stories and information.

TOM   She sounds —

EAMON   Carriages, balls, receptions, weddings, christenings, feasts, deaths, trips to Rome, musical evenings, tennis — that's the mythology I was nurtured on all my life, day after day, year after year — the life of the 'quality' — that's how she pronounces it, with a flat 'a'. A strange and marvellous education for a wee country boy, wasn't it? No, not an education — a permanent pigmentation. I'll tell you something, Professor: I know more about this place, infinitely more, here and here (*head and heart*) than they know. Sure? (*Drink*) You'll enjoy this. (*Now to* ALICE *up in the gazebo*) Telling the Professor about the night I told Granny you and I were getting married. (*To* TOM) Not a notion in the world we were going out, of course. My god, Miss Alice and her grandson! Anyhow. 'Granny,' I said this night, 'Alice and I are going to get married.' 'Alice? Who's Alice? Alice Devenny? Alice Byrne? Not Alice Smith!' 'Alice O'Donnell.' 'What Alice O'Donnell's that?' 'Alice O'Donnell of the Hall.' A long silence. Then: 'May God and His holy mother forgive you, you dirty-mouthed upstart!' (*Laughs*) Wasn't that an interesting response? As we say about here: Now you're an educated man, Professor — what do you make of that response?

TOM   Oh boy.

EAMON   'Oh boy'?

TOM   What do *you* make of it?

EAMON   Would you like to meet her?

TOM   That would be —

EAMON   I'm sure I could manage to squeeze an appointment.

TOM   Actually I'm leaving to- —

EAMON   She'd love to talk to you; I know she would.

TOM   Perhaps some other —

EAMON   She's crazy about Americans. She has a sister a waitress in the Bronx and a picture of Tom Mix above her bed. Hello, Uncle George. Sit down and give us a bit of your crack.

> *This to* UNCLE GEORGE *who has entered left — his usual entrance, finding himself in the middle of the group before he is aware that they are there. As before, he stands and stares and then retreats the way he came.*

There goes one happy man.

> CASIMIR *has hung up and now stands at the study/ lawn door.*

CASIMIR   Can't get past Letterkenny. But they'll keep trying.

EAMON	Casimir? (*Drink*)
CASIMIR	Later, perhaps. Now be patient for another few minutes and I'll bring out a beautiful picnic lunch.
CLAIRE	Do you need any help?
CASIMIR	Me? Didn't I tell you what the boys call me? The Kindermädchen.
CLAIRE	What's that? (*To* TOM) What does that mean?
TOM	Is it the — children's maid? The nanny?
CASIMIR	Well, yes, I suppose that's the literal translation but in this context it means — it means — well, it's really a kind of comical, affectionate term. They like to pull my leg, you know. Contrary to popular opinion the German temperament is naturally very — very frivolous and very, *very* affectionate. Where's Alice?
ALICE	Hello.
CASIMIR	What are you hiding there for?
ALICE	Getting drunk.
CASIMIR	Now you're being frivolous. Right — ten minutes at the outside.

He goes back into the study and off into the hall.

TOM	The telephone system here is really unsatisfactory, isn't it?
EAMON	All a game.
TOM	In what way?
EAMON	Casimir pretending he's calling Helga the Hun. All a game. All a fiction.
ALICE	Oh shut up!
EAMON	No one has ever seen her. We're convinced he's invented her.

TOM *laughs uncertainly.*

TOM	Is he serious, Claire?
EAMON	And the three boys — Herbert, Hans and Heinrich. And the dachshund bitch called Dietrich. And his job in the sausage factory. It has the authentic ring of phoney fiction, hasn't it?

CLAIRE   Don't listen to him, Tom.

> ALICE *has come down from the gazebo to fill her glass.*

ALICE   What's your phoney fiction?

EAMON   That I'm a laughing broth of an Irish boy. (*To* TOM) What was the word you used a few minutes ago — that yoke in there — what did you call it? A baby- —?

TOM   Baby-alarm.

EAMON   That's it — baby-alarm.

TOM   You place a small microphone above a baby's cot so that if it cries —

EAMON   I know — I know how it works. No practical experience of course — have we, love? Just that I find the name curious. Good luck. Yes, I suppose baby-alarm has an aptness in the circumstances. But there's another word — what's the name I'm looking for? — What do you call the peep-hole in a prison door? Judas hole! That's it. Would that be more appropriate? But then we'd have to decide who's spying on whom, wouldn't we? No; let's keep baby-alarm. Gentler. (*Laughs*) 'Baby-alarm' — yes, I like baby-alarm. (*To* ALICE) Shouldn't you go easy on that?

ALICE   Shut up.

EAMON   (*To* TOM) Less than twenty-four hours away from temperate London and already we're reverting to drunken Paddies. Must be the environment, mustn't it? Man-a-dear but that's a powerful aul' lump of a summer's day.

> TOM *is looking at his notes.* ALICE *has gone back to the gazebo.* EAMON *crosses to* CLAIRE *who is sewing and sits beside her. He puts his arm round her.*

I'm talking too much, amn't I? (*Pause*) I always talk too much in this house, don't I? Is it because I'm still intimidated by it? (*Pause*) And this was always a house of reticence, of things unspoken, wasn't it?

	(*She looks at him and smiles. He touches her chin*) Keep your peace, little wise one. (*He removes his arm from round her*) Judith tells me I'm proposing the toast to the groom's family.
CLAIRE	You know Jerry, don't you?
EAMON	Not very well. He was that bit older. (*Aware*) Well — a few years — and when you're young it seems a lot. (*She takes his glass and drinks*) Hey! What about those pills?
CLAIRE	I haven't taken today's yet.
EAMON	Why not?
CLAIRE	You know his sister, Ellen?
EAMON	Yes.
CLAIRE	Do you like her?
EAMON	Ellen has her own ways.
CLAIRE	She'll be living in the house with Jerry and me.
EAMON	For a while, maybe. Ellen'll marry and move out.
CLAIRE	No, she won't move out. And she won't marry now — she's almost fifty-four — she's only a year younger than Jerry. And the house is hers. And yesterday she said to me that she'll carry on as usual — doing the cooking and the housework. So I'll have nothing to do. A life of leisure. Maybe take the children for walks — she suggested that. But that's all. The whole day idle. And he's getting me a car next Christmas so that I won't even have to walk. Next time you're back I'll have put on ten stone!
EAMON	I thought Jerry would want a working wife?
CLAIRE	Oh, yes. He's buying a piano so that I can teach the children to play. Maybe one of them will become a concert pianist?

She gets up and moves across the lawn.

| EAMON | What the hell's keeping Casimir with the grub? |

He rises and pours himself another drink.

God bless Willie Diver. Did you know I was his best

man? My God, *that* was a wedding. I was seventeen, Willie was eighteen, and Nora Sheridan, known locally as Nora the Nun — for reasons of Irish irony, Professor — Nora was thirty if she was a day. And at seventeen I thought: My God, lucky aul' Slooghter, marrying the village pro, my God he'll be getting it morning, noon and night and what more could a man want! But of course the marriage lasted five months and the brave Nora cleared off with a British soldier stationed in Derry and was never seen again and aul' Willie was back with the rest of us hoping to get it maybe once a year on St Patrick's night with big Tessie Mulligan if you promised to take her and her twin sister to the pig co-op dance. Isn't life full of tiny frustrations, Professor? And how's the research going?

TOM	Satisfactorily.
EAMON	Are you writing a book?
TOM	Eventually.
EAMON	About?
TOM	I'm not going to bore you with my theories.
EAMON	Please. (*To* ALICE) We're captivated — aren't we, love?
TOM	Alice is not captivated.
EAMON	Alice reveals her passion in oblique ways.
TOM	I'd really rather not —
EAMON	But I'm interested; I'm genuinely interested. Please.
TOM	Well, when we talk about the big house in this country, we usually mean the Protestant big house with its Anglo-Irish tradition and culture; and the distinction is properly made between that tradition and culture and what we might call the native Irish tradition and culture which is Roman Catholic.
EAMON	With reservations — yes. So?
TOM	So what I'm researching is the life and the lifestyle of the Roman Catholic big house — by no means as thick on the ground but still there; what we might call a Roman Catholic aristocracy — for want of a better term.
EAMON	No, no, it's a good term; I like the term. The Professor's

talking about you, love!

TOM   And the task I've set myself is to explore its political, cultural and economic influence both on the ascendancy ruling class and on the native peasant tradition. Over the past one hundred and fifty years — in fact since Catholic Emancipation — what political clout did they wield, what economic contribution did they make to the status of their co-religionists, what cultural effect did they have on the local peasantry?

EAMON   The Professor's talking about me, love! And Ballybeg Hall's your prototype?

TOM   No, just one example.

EAMON   And what conclusions have you reached?

TOM   None yet, Eamon. I'm still digging.

EAMON   Ah. Let's see can we help the Professor. What were the questions again? What political clout did they wield? (*Considers. Then sadly shakes his head*) What economic help were they to their co-religionists? (*Considers. Then sadly shakes his head*) What cultural effect did they have on the local peasantry? Alice? (*Considers. Then sadly shakes his head*) We agree, I'm afraid. Sorry, Professor. Bogus thesis. No book.

TOM   Okay. So no book.

EAMON   But you'll go ahead all the same, won't you?

TOM   I may well be so obtuse.

CASIMIR enters the study, carrying a large tray. As he crosses the lawn he chants

CASIMIR   'What we are about to receive is a magnificent lunch which will be served on the lawn and it has been prepared specially and with meticulous care by — '

He is now on the lawn and is about to put the tray on the ground when his chant is interrupted by FATHER's *clear and commanding voice.*

FATHER   Casimir!

44

CASIMIR *jumps to attention; rigid, terrified.*

CASIMIR   Yes sir!
FATHER   Come to the library at once. I wish to speak to you.

> CASIMIR *now realizes that the voice has come from the speaker.*

CASIMIR   Christ — oh-oh-oh my God — Ha-ha. Isn't that a very comical joke — I almost stood to attention — I almost stood —

> *He looks round at the others who are staring at him. He tries to smile. He is totally lost. He looks at the tray; then sinks to the ground with it, ending in a kneeling position.*

That's the second time I was caught — the second time —

> JUDITH *enters with the teapot. The eldest of the O'Donnell family: almost forty. She is dressed in old working clothes. Her appearance is of little interest to her.*

JUDITH   Did you bring the sugar and the sandwiches, Casimir? I've got the tea here.
FATHER   At once, Sir. And bring your headmaster's report with you. I intend to get to the bottom of this.
CASIMIR   Judith?
JUDITH   What is it?
CASIMIR   Judith?

> *She goes quickly outside, gets down beside him and takes him in her arms. He is crying now.*

I'm sorry — I'm sorry — I'm very sorry.
JUDITH   It's alright.
CASIMIR   I'm very sorry, very sorry.

JUDITH	Everything's alright — everything's fine.
CASIMIR	I don't think it's fair, Judith.
JUDITH	Shhhhh.
CASIMIR	That's the second time I was caught by it. It's not fair — it's not fair.
JUDITH	Shhhhh.
CASIMIR	Ha-ha. It's not fair.

She rocks him in her arms as if he were a baby. The others look away. Bring lights down slowly.

ACT TWO

About an hour later. The remains of the lunch are scattered over the lawn: dishes, linen napkins, food, some empty wine bottles.

The sun, the food, the wine have taken their toll: EAMON *is sprawled on the grass, dozing.* JUDITH, *her eyes closed, her face tilted up to the sun, is smoking a cigarette.* WILLIE *is sitting on the step immediately above and behind her.* CLAIRE *is sitting apart from the others, close to the sundial.* TOM *is in the gazebo, reading a newspaper but aware of what the others are doing.*

CASIMIR *is crawling around on his hands and knees, moving along very slowly and feeling the ground very carefully with his fingertips. He is totally concentrated on this strange task. He is looking for the holes left by croquet hoops; on the same site as the vanished tennis court.*

Only ALICE *is lively. She has had a little too much to drink and she is pacing about, glass in hand, occasionally making giddy, complicated little steps with her feet.*

ALICE   I know you're paying no attention to me — old Alice is a little tiddly, isn't she? But what I'm suggesting is very sensible. The meal will be over at half-one or two; and the happy couple will drive off into eternal bliss. And what's to become of the rest of us? Sit looking at one another with melancholy faces? Sleep? Talk about old times? Listen to Father on the baby-alarm? (*Short giggle — then remorse. To* CASIMIR) Apologies. Withdraw that. That was unkind. So what do we do? My suggestion is — no, it's a formal proposal, Madam Chairman (*Judith*) — I put it to your worship that we all head off somewhere and have some fun ourselves. You'll drive us, Willie, won't you?

WILLIE   Surely to God. Anywhere you want.

ALICE   All set, then. Where'll we go? Glencolmcille! Who's
         for —

         JUDITH *sits up very quickly and lifts the writing*
         pad at her side (her list of wedding preparations).

JUDITH   Willie isn't free to go anywhere.

         ALICE *grimaces extravagantly behind her back.*

ALICE   Oooooh. So Willie isn't free. Alright, we'll club to-
         gether and rent a car — no, *I'll* rent a car and you'll
         all be my guests. Is that a unanimous verdict?
JUDITH   Let's get back to these things.
ALICE   And we'll bring our court clerk with us and every
         word we utter will be carefully recorded.
JUDITH   Where had we got to? Any word from the photographer?
WILLIE   He'll be there at the chapel and then he'll come up
         here afterwards.
ALICE   God help the poor man if he thinks he's heard one
         word of truth since he came here. Is he in the
         library?
TOM   Careful, Alice: I'm here.
ALICE   All you're hearing is lies, my friend — lies, lies, lies.
TOM   What's the truth?
ALICE   Later in the day and alcoholic Alice'll tell all.
JUDITH   I've asked one of the Moloney girls to look after
         Father while we're at the church. Are you busy that
         morning?
WILLIE   Doing nothing.
JUDITH   Could you run her up? About half-nine?
WILLIE   No bother.
JUDITH   Thanks.
ALICE   Well, if none of you want to come with me, as
         Sister Thérèse used to say — remember her strange
         English? — 'Boo-gar the whole lot of you!'

         She slumps into a chair and closes her eyes.

JUDITH 'Food' — that's all got except for the ham.

CASIMIR Hurrah!

> CASIMIR's *sudden triumphant exclamation startles everybody.* EAMON *wakens, startled.*

There you are! Knew they were here!

EAMON God.

CASIMIR There! Look — look — look!

> *He has a finger stuck into the ground.*

ALICE Good old Casimir!

CASIMIR Now if there's one there, there must be another somewhere beside it.

> *He bends over to his search again.* EAMON *gets to his feet.*

EAMON What is he at? Who's missing?

JUDITH What's the position about the flowers, Claire?

CASIMIR Here it is! (*He stands up*) You see — I remember it. Distinctly! (*He marks the spot with a napkin*) That means that there must be another one — (*he strides across the lawn*) — somewhere about here. (*He grins at* EAMON) Amn't I right?

EAMON I'm sure you are.

CASIMIR Seven in all — isn't that it?

EAMON At least.

CASIMIR No, no, just seven; and the peg in the middle.

> *He suddenly drops on his hands and knees again and begins groping.*

EAMON Who is Peg?

JUDITH Claire!

CLAIRE Sorry?

JUDITH The flowers arrive on the last bus tomorrow night?

CLAIRE (*Vague, indifferent*) I think so.

JUDITH	And Jerry'll collect them and bring them up here?
CLAIRE	Yes — probably — I suppose so.
JUDITH	Claire, it's —
WILLIE	I'll remind him this evening.
JUDITH	Would you?
WILLIE	And if he's busy I'll collect them.

EAMON *picks up the cassette player and switches it on — Étude No.3 in E major. He sings with it in a parody of the Crosby style of the late forties.*

EAMON	'So deep is the night — '

CASIMIR, *automatically, without looking up*

CASIMIR	Terrific. The E major étude — right, Claire?
EAMON	F major.

CASIMIR *sits up.*

CASIMIR	Are you — ? No, it's the — Ah, you're taking a hand at me, Eamon! I know you are. Ha-ha. Very good. Very comical.

He bends to his search again.

EAMON	'No moon tonight; no friendly star to guide me on my way — boo-be-doo-ba-ba-de-ba — '

He pours himself a drink.

JUDITH	What arrangement have you come to with Miss Quirk, Claire?
CLAIRE	No arrangement.
JUDITH	Is she going to play or is she not?
CLAIRE	I told you all I know. I met her by accident.
JUDITH	And what did she say?
CLAIRE	All she said was 'I play the harmonium at every wedding in Ballybeg.'

ALICE   (*Eyes closed*) Who? Miss Quirk? Oh my God!

CLAIRE   I don't care. Let her play if she wants.

JUDITH   Did she ask you what music you wanted?

CLAIRE   You know very well she can play only two pieces.

ALICE   Tom Hoffnung!

TOM   Hello?

ALICE   Before you leave you should meet Miss Quirk.

TOM   Yeah?

ALICE   She's the Scott Joplin of Donegal.

JUDITH   (*To* WILLIE) I suppose I'll have to pay her something?

WILLIE   I'll look after it. You can square with me later.

> EAMON *is wandering around, glass in hand. He sings with the tape again, inventing the words he has forgotten.*

EAMON   'And so am I, lonely and forgotten by the stream —' (*To* WILLIE) Remember dancing to that in the Corinthian in Derry?

WILLIE   Every Friday night.

EAMON   The steam rising out of us from getting soaked cycling in on the bikes.

WILLIE   And the big silver ball going round and round up on the ceiling. Jaysus.

EAMON   Tommy McGee on the sax; Bobby Kyle on piano; Jackie Fogarty on drums; young Turbet on clarinet.

WILLIE   And slipping out to the cloakroom for a slug out of the bottle.

EAMON   And the long dresses — the New Look — isn't that what it was called?

WILLIE   Oh Jaysus.

EAMON   (*To* JUDITH) Remembrance of things past.

JUDITH   (*To* WILLIE) Is that coffee stone cold?

> WILLIE *rises immediately.*

WILLIE   If there's any left in it.

> *He goes to the remains of the picnic.*

EAMON	Do you remember the night we sneaked out to the Corinthian on my uncle's motor bike?
JUDITH	Yes.
EAMON	We were still sitting over there (*gazebo*) when the sun came up.
CASIMIR	Here we are! Two more holes! Corner number two! All agreed?

He stands up, marks the position with a napkin as before, and goes to another part of the lawn.

EAMON	You wore your mother's silver tiara in your hair. Do you remember?
JUDITH	Yes.
EAMON	Everything?
CASIMIR	So that number three must be about — here.

He drops on his hands and knees again and begins groping.

ALICE	(*Eyes closed*) I have it on very good authority that in the privacy of her digs Miss Quirk plays the ukulele and sings dirty songs.
EAMON	There was a hedgehog caught in the tennis net. He had rolled himself up into a ball and his spikes were up against danger. Like me, you said. Do you remember?
JUDITH	Yes.
EAMON	And I asked you to marry me.
ALICE	I'm ashamed to say I like dirty songs, Tom.
EAMON	And you said yes.
JUDITH	Where had we got to? — Taxis. What about taxis, Willie?
WILLIE	You'll need only two. The car that leaves Jerry at the chapel then comes up here for you and Claire; and it waits here until the other car has headed off with the rest of the family and then it follows on. (*He returns with a cup of coffee*) There's a wee drop in it — it's not too bad. They were good times, Eamon, eh?, them

nights in the Corinthian.

EAMON   They were good times, Professor.

TOM   What were?

EAMON   Plebeian past times. Before we were educated out of our emotions.

He switches up the volume of the cassette while he sings again.

'So deep is the night, ba-ba-dee-boo-ba-ba-ba-ba — '

He reduces the volume again.

JUDITH   I think we have enough wine.

ALICE   I hope there's plenty wine.

WILLIE   (*To* ALICE) I left in two cases — is that enough?

ALICE *now opens her eyes and sits forward.*

ALICE   Good ole Willie! (*Sings*) 'Drink to me only with thine eyes — '

Immediately EAMON *begins singing.*

EAMON   'Boo-ba-de-boo-ba-ba — '

ALICE   'And I will pledge with mine.'

CASIMIR, *without interrupting his search, joins* ALICE.

'Or leave a kiss but in the cup
And I'll not look for wine.'

ALICE *sits back, closes her eyes and continues humming.*

EAMON   (*To* TOM) Recognize it?

TOM   Elizabethan. Is it Ben Jonson?

EAMON   The very buck. Used to nip into the scullery and

	recite it to Granny.
TOM	I think perhaps I should check that.
EAMON	Would I tell you a lie?
FATHER	I have considered very carefully everything I have heard and I must now ask you to — I must request — I must — I — I —

The suddenness and authority of FATHER's *voice create a stillness, almost an unease. Nobody speaks for a few seconds.*

JUDITH	He's very restless today.
CASIMIR	I wasn't caught that time — no, no! I wasn't caught that time — ha-ha!
FATHER	Judith!

CASIMIR *stiffens.*

	Judith? Judith? Where's Judith? Jud-ith!
ALICE	Stay where you are. I'll go. (*She rises*)
JUDITH	It's alright. He probably wants nothing at all.

JUDITH *goes off quickly.* ALICE *walks about. She is slightly unsteady.*

| ALICE | But I would like to go — I would like to help. Why won't she let me help? When I went up to see him last night just after I arrived, I got such a shock — he's so altered. Isn't he altered? I mean he was always such a big strong man with such power, such authority; and then to see him lying there, so flat under the clothes, with his mouth open — |

CASIMIR *stands up. He has been listening to* ALICE *and the vigour of his announcement this time is forced.*

| CASIMIR | The third! There you are! Number three! (*He marks it as before*) Only one more to get. |

He crosses the lawn to the fourth corner but does not go down on his hands and knees. He stands listening to ALICE.

ALICE　I caught his face between my hands — isn't that right, Casimir? You were there beside me — and I held it like that. And it was such a strange sensation — I must never have touched his face before — is that possible never to have touched my father's face? And it seemed so small between my hands; and it was so cool and his beard so rough and I felt so — so equal to him. (*She begins to cry*) And then he opened his eyes. And he didn't recognize me — isn't that right, Casimir? And that's when I began to cry. He didn't know me. He didn't know you, either, Casimir, did he?

CASIMIR　No.

ALICE　He didn't know me either. It was so strange — your own father, not knowing you. He didn't know you either, Casimir, did he?

CASIMIR　No.

ALICE　His own flesh and blood. Did he know you, Willie?

WILLIE　Well, you see like, Alice, I'm not his son.

ALICE　That's true. And that's when I began to cry. I'm sorry — I'm sorry — I know I'm slightly drunk but I'm still capable of — of — of —

EAMON *offers her Judith's coffee — she brushes past him.*

I want a drink. Who's hidden the drink? Where's the drink all hidden? (*She finds it and helps herself*) Oh dear, dear God.

EAMON　'Boo-ba-de-ba-ba-ba-ba; boom-boom-boom.'

EAMON *moves over beside* CLAIRE. CASIMIR *gets down on his hands and knees again.* ALICE *drops into a seat and closes her eyes.*

	Whatever he's looking for, he deserves to find it.
CLAIRE	The remains of an old croquet court.
EAMON	Ah. Before my time.

A new tape begins: Nocturne in F sharp major, Op.15 No.2. CLAIRE *is fingering a gold watch.*

	Present from Jerry?
CLAIRE	For my last birthday.
EAMON	Very handsome, isn't it?
JUDITH	Is something wrong?
CLAIRE	Yes.
FATHER	Judith?
JUDITH	I'm here beside you.
CLAIRE	And I told you, didn't I — he's getting me a car for Christmas.
JUDITH	What's the matter?
EAMON	Lucky you.
FATHER	Judith?
JUDITH	What is it?
CLAIRE	And he's had the whole house done up from top to bottom. New carpets everywhere — even in the kitchen. I helped Ellen choose them.
JUDITH	Are you cold? Do you want the quilt on again?

Without any change in her tone, and smiling as if she were chatting casually, CLAIRE *continues.*

CLAIRE	I'm in a mess, Eamon.
JUDITH	You're upset today.
CLAIRE	I don't know if I can go on with it.
JUDITH	You got your pills, didn't you?
FATHER	Judith betrayed the family — did you know that?
JUDITH	Yes. Now — that's better.
FATHER	Great betrayal; enormous betrayal.
JUDITH	Let me feel those tops.
FATHER	But Anna's praying for her. Did you know that?
JUDITH	Yes, I know that, Father.
CLAIRE	Listen to them! (*Short laugh*) It goes on like that all

	the time, all the time. I don't know how Judith stands it. She's lucky to be so — so strong minded. Sometimes I think it's driving me mad. Mustn't it have been something trivial like that that finally drove Mother to despair? And then sometimes I think: I'm going to miss it so much. I'm so confused, Eamon.
EAMON	Aren't we all confused?
CLAIRE	But if you really loved someone the way you're supposed to love someone you're about to marry, you shouldn't be confused, should you? Everything should be absorbed in that love, shouldn't it? There'd be no reservations, would there? I'd love his children and his sister and his lorry and his vegetables and his carpets and everything, wouldn't I? And I'd love all of him, too, wouldn't I?

EAMON *puts his arm round her.*

	That's one of the last nocturnes he wrote.
EAMON	Is it?
CLAIRE	Why does he not see that I'm in a mess, Eamon?
EAMON	You don't have to go on with it, you know.

CASIMIR *is suddenly and triumphantly on his feet again.*

| CASIMIR | Number four! There you are! The complete croquet court! See, Eamon? Look, Claire! I remember! I knew! |

CLAIRE *jumps up. She is suddenly vigorous, buoyant, excited. Her speech is rapid.*

CLAIRE	Come on — who's for a game?
CASIMIR	Me-me-me!
CLAIRE	Give me a mallet.

CASIMIR *mimes giving her one.*

CASIMIR	There you are.
CLAIRE	Is this the best you have?
CASIMIR	It's brand new — never been used.
CLAIRE	Where are the hoops?
CASIMIR	All in position. Just a second. (*He drops three more napkins in the centre of the court*) That's it. This one (*centre napkin*) is the peg.
CLAIRE	And the balls?
CASIMIR	At your feet.
CLAIRE	Right.
CASIMIR	Who goes first?
CLAIRE	The bride-to-be — who else?
CASIMIR	Wonderful! Off you go. Ladies and gentlemen — please — give the players room. Thank you. Thank you.
CLAIRE	First shot of the game.
CASIMIR	And a beautiful, beautiful shot it is. Now for the champion.

> *This imaginary game and their exchanges about it continue during the following sequences.* EAMON *rises; switches off the cassette; picks up a bottle of wine and a glass; drifts across the lawn. As he passes* WILLIE

EAMON	'Ba-ba-de-boo-ba-ba.' Many hedgehogs about now?
WILLIE	What?
EAMON	Hedgehogs — you know — (*he mimes one*) — many of them about?
WILLIE	How the hell would I know about hedgehogs?
EAMON	'Ba-ba-de-boo-ba-ba — Ba-ba-boo — '
WILLIE	Hedgehogs! Jaysus!

> WILLIE *goes to the croquet court and watches the game.*

CASIMIR	That was good — that was very good.
CLAIRE	That was brilliant.
CASIMIR	But watch this. This is how it's really done. Aaaaaah!

58

ALICE *opens her eyes, sits forward, and watches*
CLAIRE *and* CASIMIR *in bewilderment.*

CLAIRE That ball hit your leg.

CASIMIR It did not.

CLAIRE I saw it — you winced.

CASIMIR (*To* ALICE) Did the ball hit my leg?

ALICE What?

CASIMIR Did you see me wince?

CLAIRE You did. I saw you. I saw you.

ALICE What are you doing?

CASIMIR Croquet. (*To* CLAIRE) My turn — right?

CLAIRE I'll let you off this time. (*To* ALICE) Keep an eye on him — he cheats.

ALICE Where are the — ?

CLAIRE But he's still not winning. (*To* CASIMIR) And watch where you're swinging that mallet.

ALICE Oh my God.

She closes her eyes and sinks back in her seat. The game continues. UNCLE GEORGE *enters the study — his usual entrance — and is out on the lawn before he discovers it is occupied. He stops, looks around.*

WILLIE Hello, Mr George.

UNCLE GEORGE *goes back into the study — and off.*

EAMON Hello, Uncle George. Goodbye, Uncle George. Not one of you is aware that on the day of our wedding Uncle George shook my hand and spoke seven words. And the seven words he spoke were: 'There's going to be a great revolution.' And I thought that after all those years of silence and contemplation that must be a profound remark. (EAMON *is now beside* TOM. *He sits very close to him and smiles warmly at him*) Wasn't I a fool?

TOM Were you?

59

EAMON	I'm wiser now.
TOM	Good.
EAMON	And I've solved your problem.
TOM	Which one's that, Eamon?
EAMON	Your book.
TOM	Have I a problem?
EAMON	It has to be a fiction — a romantic fiction — like Helga the Hun.
TOM	Yeah?
EAMON	A great big blockbuster of a Gothic novel called *Ballybeg Hall — From Supreme Court to Sausage Factory*; four generations of a great Irish Catholic legal dynasty; the gripping saga of a family that lived its life in total isolation in a gaunt Georgian house on top of a hill above the remote Donegal village of Ballybeg; a family without passion, without loyalty, without commitments; administering the law for anyone who happened to be in power; above all wars and famines and civil strife and political upheaval; ignored by its Protestant counterparts, isolated from the mere Irish, existing only in its own concept of itself, brushing against reality occasionally by its cultivation of artists; but tough — oh, yes, tough, resilient, tenacious; and with one enormous talent for — no, a *greed* for survival — that's the family motto, isn't it? — *Semper Permanemus.* Don't for a second underestimate them. What do you think?
TOM	It's your fiction.
EAMON	A bit turgid — yes — I can see that. (*Suddenly happy again*) But the romantic possibilities are there — oh, yes, by God. Mother, for example. Make Mother central.
ALICE	Leave Mother out of it.
EAMON	Why?
ALICE	You really are a bastard!
EAMON	Because I see Mother as central?
ALICE	For Christ's sake!
EAMON	Trust me — I'm an ex-diplomat.
ALICE	Trust you!

60

EAMON Yes, I have pieties, too. (*To* TOM) She was an actress.
Did you know that? No, you didn't — that little
detail was absorbed into the great silence. Yes;
travelling round the country with the Charles Doran
Company. Spotted by the judge in the lounge of the
Railway Hotel and within five days decently wed
and ensconced in the Hall here and bugger poor aul'
Charles Doran who had to face the rest of rural
Ireland without a Colleen Bawn! And a raving
beauty by all accounts. No sooner did Yeats clap
eyes on her than a sonnet burst from him — 'That I
may know the beauty of that form' — Alice'll rattle
it off for you there. Oh, terrific stuff. And O'Casey —
haven't they told you that one? — poor O'Casey out
here one day ploughterin' after tennis balls and
spoutin' about the workin'-man when she appeared
in the doorway in there and the poor creatur' made
such a ram-stam to get to her that he tripped over
the Pope or Plato or Shirley Temple or somebody
and smashed his bloody glasses! The more you think
of it — all those calamities — Chesterton's ribs,
Hopkins's hand, O'Casey's aul' specs — the County
Council should put up a sign outside that room —
Accident Black Spot — shouldn't they? Between
ourselves, it's a very dangerous house, Professor.

TOM What have you got against me, Eamon?

EAMON And of course you'll have chapters on each of the
O'Donnell forebears: Great Grandfather — Lord
Chief Justice; Grandfather — Circuit Court Judge;
Father — simple District Justice; Casimir — failed
solicitor. A fairly rapid descent; but no matter, no
matter; good for the book; failure's more lovable
than success. D'you know, Professor, I've often
wondered: if we had had children and they wanted
to be part of the family legal tradition, the only
option open to them would have been as criminals,
wouldn't it? (*Offering the bottle*) There's enough here
for both of us. No? (*He pours a drink for himself*) After
we went upstairs last night, Alice and I, we had

words, as they say. She threw a book at me. And I struck her. You've noticed her cheek, haven't you? No one else here would dream of commenting on it; but you did, didn't you? And she didn't tell you, did she? Of course she didn't. That's why she's freezing me. But she'll come round. It'll be absorbed. Duty'll conquer.

TOM I don't want to hear about your —

EAMON What have I got against you?

TOM Yes. You're the only member of the family who has been — less than courteous to me since I came here. I don't know why that is. I guess you resent me for some reason.

EAMON *considers this. He is not smiling now.*

EAMON Nervous; that's all. In case — you'll forgive me — in case you're not equal to your task. In case you'll loot and run. Nervous that all you'll see is (*indicates the croquet game*) — the make-believe.

JUDITH *enters the study. As she does, the phone rings. She answers it.*

No, I don't resent you, Professor. I'm sure you're an honest recorder. I'm nervous of us; we don't pose to our best advantage.

JUDITH Casimir!

CASIMIR Hello?

CLAIRE I have you on the run now.

CASIMIR You certainly have not.

JUDITH Phone, Casimir!

His usual response to this.

CASIMIR The phone! — Helga — That'll be Helga — sorry — sorry — excuse me — sorry —

As he rushes into the study he trips on the step.

62

I beg your pardon — forgive me —

He rushes on in.

CLAIRE You play for him until he comes back, Willie.
WILLIE Me?
CLAIRE There's nothing to it.
WILLIE Aw, g'way out of that.
CLAIRE Come on. You start over there.
WILLIE Sure I mean to say —
CLAIRE You aim for that post first and then you drive the ball through the hoop over in that far corner.
CASIMIR Hello? Hello? Hello?

> WILLIE *looks round at the others. He is embarrassed and afraid of being laughed at — particularly by* EAMON — *so he laughs foolishly.*

WILLIE Me playing croquet — and nothing to play with! Jaysus! Sure I never even seen the game in my —
CLAIRE You've been watching us, haven't you? (*Thrusts a mallet into his hand*) Go on! All you do is hit the ball. It's very simple.
WILLIE All the same you feel a bit of an eejit — (*To* EAMON) They have me playing croquet now, Eamon! Without balls nor nothin'! Jaysus!
EAMON Go ahead, William. Take the plunge. Submit to baptism. You'll never look back.
WILLIE I couldn't —
CLAIRE If you're going to play, will you play!
CASIMIR Halloh? Halloh? Helga? Wer spricht dort, bitte?

> WILLIE *hesitates. Then suddenly flings off his jacket, spits on his hands and rubs them together.*

WILLIE Right — right — I'll play — indeed and I'll play — where's the ball? — Give us a mallet — out of my road — where do I begin? Let me at it.

As before keep up the dialogue during the CLAIRE/
WILLIE *game.* JUDITH, *who has been tidying in the*
study, now comes out.

EAMON   How is he?

JUDITH   Alright, I think. It might be just the heat. (*He gives her*
his glass) What about you?

He looks around — finds another.

EAMON   Here we are.

CLAIRE   Very good, Willie. You're getting the hang of it.

WILLIE   Am I? By Jaysus maybe I am too.

EAMON *sits beside* JUDITH. *She is aware he is looking*
at her.

JUDITH   It's almost warm. (*Pause*) I get sleepy if I take more
than one glass. (*Pause*) This must be my third today.

ALICE *moves in her seat.*

ALICE   Oh, that's very nice.

JUDITH   She's got older looking.

EAMON   Yes.

JUDITH   Has it become a real problem?

EAMON   When is a problem a real problem?

JUDITH   I suppose when you can't control it.

EAMON   She was fine until November, dry for almost eighteen months. Since then she's been in hospital twice.
And I knew this trip would be a disaster.

JUDITH   I tried to talk to her last night —

EAMON   About her drinking?

JUDITH   No, no; about London. I was suggesting she get a
job. She said none of us was trained to do anything.
And she's right — we're not. Anyhow she cut me
off. But she was always closer to Claire; and Casimir,
of course.

EAMON   We live in a damp basement flat about half the size

	of the morning room, I'm out all day and a lot of nights. It's a very lonely life for her. You'll miss Claire.
JUDITH	Yes.
EAMON	She won't be far away.
JUDITH	That's true.
EAMON	Just you and Father.
JUDITH	And Uncle George.
EAMON	And Uncle George.
JUDITH	Yes.
EAMON	It'll be a quiet house.
JUDITH	We manage.
WILLIE	Go on — go on — go on — go on — go on.
EAMON	You said that morning you'd marry me.
JUDITH	We manage because we live very frugally. There's Father's pension; and I get some money from letting the land; and I grow all the vegetables we use; and I enjoy baking —
EAMON	Why did you change your mind?
JUDITH	So that apart from doctors' bills the only expenses we have are fuel and electric and the phone. And I'm thinking of getting rid of the phone. It's used very little anyhow.
EAMON	You never told me why.
WILLIE	You missed it! You missed it!
CLAIRE	I did not!
WILLIE	You weren't within a bloody mile of it! Ha-ha-ha-ha.
JUDITH	And I have Willie. I don't think I could manage without Willie's help. Yes, I probably could. Yes, of course I would. But he's the most undemanding person I know. Some intuitive sense he has: he's always there when I want him. And everything he does is done so simply, so easily, that I almost take him for granted.
EAMON	Judith, I —

She closes her eyes and her speech becomes tense and deliberate, almost as if she were talking to herself.

JUDITH   Listen to me, Eamon. I get up every morning at 7.30 and make breakfast. I bring Father his up first. Very often the bed's soiled so I change him and sponge him and bring the clothes downstairs and wash them and hang them out. Then I get Uncle George his breakfast. Then I let the hens out and dig the potatoes for the lunch. By that time Claire's usually up so I get her something to eat and if she's in one of her down times I invent some light work for her to do, just to jolly her along, and if she's in one of her high times I've got to try to stop her from scrubbing down the house from top to bottom. Then I do out the fire, bring in the turf, make the beds, wash the dishes. Then it's time to bring Father up his egg-flip and shave him and maybe change his clothes again. Then I begin the lunch. And so it goes on and on, day after day, week after week, month after month. I'm not complaining, Eamon. I'm just telling you my routine. I don't even think of it as burdensome. But it occupies every waking moment of every day and every thought of every day. And I know I can carry on — happily almost, yes almost happily — I know I can keep going as long as I'm not diverted from that routine, as long as there are no intrusions on it. Maybe it's an unnatural existence. I don't know. But it's my existence — here — now. And there is no end in sight. So please don't intrude on it. Keep out of it. Now. Altogether. Please.

         She lights a cigarette. Pause.

EAMON   Whatever the lady wants.

         TOM *joins them.* EAMON *rises and flashes a radiant smile at him.*

         Semper Permanemus. (*Almost into* TOM's *face as he shuffles past him*) 'Ba-doo-be-da-da-da-ba-dab — '

TOM *ignores him. He picks up an empty wine bottle and examines it with excessive interest.*

TOM   I've some packing to do. Thank Casimir for lunch, will you?

JUDITH   Yes.

TOM   I'd be careful of that sun. You should have your head covered.

He goes off right. WILLIE *is down on his hunkers, fanning an imaginary ball through an imaginary hoop.*

WILLIE   Come on, my wee darling, come on, come on, come on, another inch, another wee fraction — And it's through! I've won! I've won!

He is elated with his triumph. His elation is genuine — not part of the make-believe. And his triumph has given him a confidence. He reaches for his jacket and swaggers off the court with great assurance.

CLAIRE   It's not over yet.

WILLIE   Over! Finished! You're bet! Pack it in! I won, Eamon!

CLAIRE   I've one more shot —

WILLIE   Bet to the ropes! Your tongue's hanging out! Throw in the towel! Aul' Slooghter won hands down! Up the back shore boys!

CLAIRE   Watch this, Willie.

WILLIE   I'm watching nothing! The game's over! (*To* EAMON) What do you make of that, lad, eh?

EAMON   'So deep is the n-n-n-n-n-night — '

CLAIRE   It's through, Willie.

WILLIE   Takes an aul' Diver every time!

ALICE is awakened by the noise. WILLIE *pursues* EAMON.

	Never had a mallet in my hand before! Never stood on a croquet court before! Bloody good, eh?
EAMON	'Terrific.' (*He gives one of Casimir's grins*) A real insider now, Willie.
WILLIE	Give us a slug of something there — I'm as dry as a lime-kiln. What's in that?

EAMON *hands him the empty wine bottle.*

EAMON	Here.
WILLIE	Jaysus, that's empty!
EAMON	Imagine it's full. Use your peasant talent for fantasy, man.

CASIMIR *has finished his call. He comes outside. He is uneasy but tries to hide it.*

CASIMIR	Well. That's that job done. Glad to get that off my mind. What's been happening out here?
JUDITH	Did you get through?
CASIMIR	Little Heinrich I was speaking to actually — he's the baby — he's seven — little Heinrich. Helga's out at one of her S G meetings. Ha-ha.
ALICE	What's her S G?
CASIMIR	The Spiritualisten Gruppe — she's a spiritualist, Helga — table-rapping, seances, all that stuff — total believer. They meet every fortnight; and they're so passionate about it — oh, my goodness, you've no idea how passionate. I pretend I'm sympathetic — you know — domestic harmony — ha-ha. So that's where she is now — at her S G meeting.
JUDITH	I'm sure Heinrich misses you.
CASIMIR	Oh yes — oh yes. But the line was bad. And the trouble is, you see, the trouble is his English is as bad as my German — if that's possible! No problem, no problem at all when we're together — I mean we can smile and make signs and stagger on; but it's so difficult on the phone. And of course Helga's right — I mean they've got to be a little German family,

haven't they? After all they're German, aren't they? So. Yes, they're all fine, thank goodness. Fine. He said to tell you all 'Grüsse' — that's the German for — for 'regards' — 'salutations' — oh, he's a very intelligent young man; very independent; very self-contained. I really must make one more big effort with my German.

JUDITH   Time we cleared this mess up.

CASIMIR   No, no; not yet. I've a great treat for all of you — Anna's tape.

ALICE   I forgot about that.

CASIMIR   Could you all gather round and I'll play the tape Anna sent me last Christmas. Messages for everybody! A real, real treat!

WILLIE   Maybe I should go and leave yous to —

CASIMIR   Go? For heaven's sake! I'd be deeply offended if you left. And so would Anna.

He begins to arrange the seats in a wide arc facing out. The others help him and begin picking up the remains of the picnic. As they do this work the following passages overlap.

JUDITH   (*To* CLAIRE) What tape is this?

CLAIRE   I don't know. Never heard of it.

ALICE   (*To* WILLIE) How did it go?

WILLIE   What?

ALICE   That mad game you were playing.

WILLIE   I won.

ALICE   How do you know when you lose?

CASIMIR   Would you sit here, Eamon?

EAMON   Anywhere you like.

CASIMIR   Splendid. Where's Tom?

JUDITH   Gone to do some packing. He said thank you for the lunch.

CASIMIR   I don't suppose he'd be very interested. (*As he switches tapes*) Disposing of you temporarily, Claire. But don't worry — we'll reinstate you.

69

Everyone is in position. CASIMIR *stands before them, the cassette in his hand. He is happy to be master of ceremonies.*

	Good. Fine. Splendid. Are we all settled? Well, before I begin, may I explain to our guest here —
CLAIRE	Who's the guest?
ALICE	I'm the guest.
CASIMIR	Willie's our guest — and a very welcome guest he is, too. (ALICE *claps*) And I just wish to explain to him that little Anna joined the convent twenty years ago, when she was only seventeen —
ALICE	Eighteen.
CASIMIR	— and that apart from one visit home she's been in Africa ever since; so that her knowledge of our lives is perhaps slightly — hasn't kept pace perhaps with the way —
ALICE	For God's sake just play it, Casimir.
CASIMIR	Yes. Ah. Yes. Play it. Indeed I —
JUDITH	Shhhhh!
CLAIRE	What?
JUDITH	Listen! (*They all listen for a moment*) Sorry. Thought I heard Father. Go ahead.
CASIMIR	Should I get Uncle George out?
ALICE	Casimir!
CASIMIR	Sorry — sorry — no point at all, is there? Yes. Are we all ready? Splendid. Sister John Henry. Little Anna.

He places the cassette player on the lawn and switches it on. ANNA's *voice is a child's voice. She speaks slowly and distinctly as if she were reading from a school book.*

ANNA	Hello Daddy and Judith and Alice and Casimir and little Claire.
ALICE	Hello, Anna.
ANNA	This is Anna speaking to you all the way from St Joseph's mission in Kuala in Zambia. I hope you are all together when this is being played because I am

imagining you all sitting before a big log fire in the drawing room — Daddy spread out and enjoying his well-earned relaxation after his strenuous day in court and the rest of you sitting on the rug or around the Christmas tree in the north window.

> ALICE *has been trying to attract* CLAIRE's *attention — she wants her glass refilled, but* CLAIRE *does not notice her. Finally, she has to whisper.*

ALICE   Claire.

CASIMIR   Shhh.

ALICE   Just a drop.

> CLAIRE *fills the glass.*

ANNA   How are you all? May I wish each and every one of you — and you, too, dear Nanny — are you there, Nanny?

ALICE   Sorry, sister.

ANNA   — may I wish you all a holy and happy Christmas and all of God's peace and content for the new year.

ALICE   Amen.

ANNA   Later in the tape Reverend Mother who is here beside me will say a few words to you and after that you will hear my school choir singing some Irish songs that I have taught them —

ALICE   God!

ANNA   — and some African songs they have taught me.

ALICE   Good God!

ANNA   I hope you will enjoy them. But first I wish to speak to my own dear Daddy. How are you, Daddy? I ought to be cross with you for never writing to me but I know how busy you always are providing for us, and Judith tells me in her letters that you are in very good health. So thank God for that.

> FATHER *enters the study. An emaciated man; eyes distraught; one arm limp; his mouth pulled down at*

one corner. A grotesque and frightening figure. He is dressed only in pyjamas. The tops are buttoned wrongly and hang off his shoulders; the bottoms about to slip off his waist. He moves very slowly — one step at a time — through the study. He is trying to locate where ANNA's *voice is coming from — his distraught eyes are rolling round the room. When he speaks his voice is barely audible.*

FATHER   Anna?

ANNA   But before I go any further, I'm going to play the violin for you — a little piece you always liked me to play for you: The Gartan Mother's Lullaby. Do you remember it?

FATHER   (*Slightly louder*) Anna?

ANNA   So this is my Christmas present to you, my dear Daddy. I hope you like it.

She plays a few bars of the music — the playing of a child. Now FATHER *is almost at the study door. He raises his head and emits an almost-animal roar.*

FATHER   Annaaaaaaaaaaaa!

The listeners outside do not react for a second. Then they panic. ALICE *grabs the machine to switch it off — and instead turns the volume up so that the tape's scream and* FATHER's *roar overlap for a few seconds. They all leap to their feet — chairs are overturned — but seem to be incapable of action.* CASIMIR *is on his knees, transfixed, immobile.* CLAIRE *is on the point of hysteria.* FATHER's *roar stops. Saliva is dribbling from his mouth. He begins to sink to the ground.* EAMON, *who is furthest away from him, is the first to move. He runs to* FATHER *and catches him as he collapses so that they both sink to the ground together. Now the tape is silenced.*

EAMON *screams at the others — screams as if his own life depended on it.*

EAMON Doctor! Call the doctor! For Christ's sake, will someone call the doctor!

Blackout.

ACT THREE

Early afternoon two days later. The seats and deckchairs as before.

EAMON *is sitting on the step.* TOM *is changing the film in his camera.* CASIMIR, *his hands behind his back, is restlessly pacing round the perimeter of the tennis court. All three are dressed in lounge suits — they have recently returned from Father's funeral.*

We can hear CLAIRE *playing the piano — Sonata No.2 in B minor, Op.35, middle section of third movement (i.e. portion between 'Dead March' statements — omit 'Dead March'). It will be necessary to repeat this music which runs up to the entrance of* ALICE *and* JUDITH.

CASIMIR   (*Pacing*) He was by no means a skilful tennis player, Father, but oh my goodness he was very consistent and very determined. (*Halts*) Alice and I would be over there and he would be here. And before he served he always went through a long ritual of placing his toe precisely on the edge of the line (*he demonstrates*), moving it and adjusting it for maybe twenty seconds until he had it exactly where he wanted it — as if the whole game depended on the exact placing of his toe. (*Paces again*) And of course this always sent Alice and me into fits of secret giggling, so that when he finally did serve, we were never able to return the ball and so he thought he was a much better player than he really was! Yes. Wonderful, wasn't it? (*Halts*) Oh but God help you if he caught you laughing — oh-ho-ho-ho. (*Paces again*) Just about this time we should all have been sitting down at the wedding reception (*looks at watch*) — yes, just about now. Funny, isn't it? The Minor Sonata — that was Grandfather O'Donnell's favourite. Probably because he actually heard Chopin play it.

74

TOM   Who heard Chopin?
CASIMIR   Grandfather. Haven't I told you that story?
TOM   No.

           CASIMIR *comes downstage.*

CASIMIR   Oh, yes. At a party in Vienna — a birthday party for
           Balzac. Everybody was there: Liszt and George
           Sand and Turgenev and Mendelssohn and the young
           Wagner and Berlioz and Delacroix and Verdi — and
           of course Balzac. Everybody. It went on for days.
           God knows why Grandfather was there — probably
           gate crashed. Anyhow that's what Chopin played.
TOM   Your grandfather, Casimir?
CASIMIR   Grandfather O'Donnell; a great traveller; Europe
           every year.
TOM   But he wouldn't have been a contemporary of these
           people, would he?
CASIMIR   Would he not?
TOM   You must mean your great-grandfather, don't you?
CASIMIR   Do I? Great-grandfather O'Donnell then. Yes, you're
           right: he lived in Europe for six months one time to
           escape the fever that followed the famine here. A
           party in Vienna. The expression became part of the
           family language: anything great and romantic and
           exciting that had happened in the past or might
           happen in the future, we called it 'a party in Vienna'
           — yes. Very beautiful, isn't it? And there was another
           detail about that party: Chopin was playing that
           sonata and Balzac began to sing it and Grandfather
           told Balzac to shut up and Chopin said, 'Bravo,
           Irishman! Bravo!' Grandfather, of course, was thrilled.
           Isn't it beautiful, Eamon?
EAMON   Yes.
CASIMIR   (*Pacing again*) Chopin died in Paris, you know, and
           when they were burying him they sprinkled Polish
           soil on his grave. (*Pause*) Because he was Polish. Did
           you notice how she went straight to the piano the
           moment we came back? Like a homing instinct; yes.

I often wonder how far she might have gone if Father hadn't thwarted her. Oh, I'm afraid he was more than naughty about that; oh, yes. Oh, I'm afraid he was adept at stifling things. I'm grateful to you for staying over, Tom.

TOM   Not at all.

CASIMIR   I appreciate it very much.

TOM   The least I could do.

CASIMIR   Is your father dead?

TOM   Yeah.

CASIMIR goes to him and very formally shakes his hand.

CASIMIR   I'm very, very sorry.

TOM   Thank you.

CASIMIR   It is a great loss.

TOM   Indeed.

CASIMIR   When did he die?

TOM   When I was three months old.

CASIMIR   Good Lord.

He begins pacing again.

TOM   A few details, Casimir; perhaps you could help me with them?

CASIMIR   Yes?

TOM   You mentioned that your mother played the piano — (*producing notebook*) — where are we? — Yeah — you talked about her playing a waltz at bedtime.

CASIMIR   The E sharp major — oh, yes, that's *my* favourite; that's easily my favourite.

TOM   You're sure about that?

CASIMIR   That The Bedtime's the E sharp major? Oh, I'm —

TOM   No, no; that your mother did play the piano.

CASIMIR halts.

Just that I inferred from something Judith said in

	passing that your mother did not in fact play.
CASIMIR	Judith said that?
TOM	What I understood was —
CASIMIR	You must have taken her up wrong, Tom. Oh, yes, Mother was a splendid pianist. By no means as talented as little Claire; but very competent. And a lovely singer. Oh, yes. Her favourite piece was a song called 'Sweet Alice'. And Father hated it — hated it. 'Rubbish,' he called it. 'Vulgar rubbish.' So that she never sang it when he was around. Oh, yes, she had lots of songs like that from her childhood. Do you know that song, Eamon?
EAMON	(*Sings*) 'Do you remember — '

CASIMIR *joins him*

'— Sweet Alice, Ben Bolt?
Sweet Alice with hair so brown?'

CASIMIR   That's it — that's it! It's not insensitive of us to sing just after Father's funeral, is it? Ha-ha. Anyway. I remember when she'd sing 'Sweet Alice' she seemed to become very, very young again and very, very beautiful, as if the song restored to her something she had lost, something that had withered in her — Oh, yes, she was a very talented pianist.

TOM   I'm sure I misunderstood Judith. It's of no importance. I'll check it again. And the other query was —

He consults his notebook again; hesitates; decides not to pursue the enquiry; closes the book and puts it in his pocket.

Yeah; that's okay; that can wait, too. No more problems.

CASIMIR   What was the other query?
TOM   Question mark after Yeats; that's all.
CASIMIR   What about him?
TOM   Just that you said you remember him sitting in —
CASIMIR   Oh my goodness yes; oh, he was just tremendous,

	Yeats, with those cold, cold eyes of his. Oh, yes, I remember Yeats vividly.
TOM	Sure.
CASIMIR	What's the question mark for?
TOM	It's of no significance. I think I got myself a little confused here, too. Doesn't matter.
CASIMIR	What's the confusion?

The music stops. TOM *produces his notebook again.*

TOM	Well, you were born on April 1, 1939.
CASIMIR	Good heavens — don't I know! All Fools' Day! Yes?
TOM	And Yeats died the same year. Two months earlier. I've double-checked it. (*He looks up from his notes.* CASIMIR *is staring at him. Pause*) I make little mistakes like that all the time myself. My mother worked for the Bell Telephone Company and until I went to High School I thought she worked for a Mr Bell who was my uncle for God's sake — It's a natural mis-understanding, that's all — I mean a man like Yeats is a visitor to your home, a friend of the family, you hear a lot of talk about him, and naturally after a time, naturally you come to think you actually — I've some correspondence to catch up with. Forgive me.

He goes into the study and off. CASIMIR *grimaces at* EAMON.

| CASIMIR | Ha-ha. It was very kind of Tom to stay over. I appreciate that very much. (*Begins pacing again*) Father would have been so pleased by that funeral today — no, not pleased — gratified, immensely gratified. The packed chapel; the music; that young curate's fine, generous panegyric, and he didn't know Father at all, Judith says. Then down through the village street — his village, his Ballybeg — that's how he thought of it, you know, and in a sense it was his village. Did you know that it used to be called O'Donnellstown? Yes, years and years ago. |

How simple it all was this time, wasn't it? You remember Mother's funeral, don't you? — all that furtiveness, all that whispering, all those half-truths. We didn't know until the very last minute would they allow her a Christian burial at all because of the circumstances — remember? But today it was — today was almost — festive by comparison, wasn't it? Every shop shut and every blind drawn; and men kneeling on their caps as the hearse passed; and Nanny sobbing her heart out when the coffin was being lowered — did you see her? — of course you did — you were beside her. All that happened, didn't it, Eamon? All that happened? Oh, yes, he would have been so gratified.

EAMON   There are certain things, certain truths, Casimir, that are beyond Tom's kind of scrutiny.

The same sonata music begins again.

CASIMIR   Oh, there are. Oh, yes, there are — aren't there? Yes — yes. I discovered a great truth when I was nine. No, not a great truth; but I made a great discovery when I was nine — not even a great discovery but an important, a very important discovery for me. I suddenly realized I was different from other boys. When I say I was different I don't mean — you know — good Lord I don't for a second mean I was — you know — as they say nowadays 'homo sexual' — good heavens I must admit, if anything, Eamon, if anything I'm — (*looks around*) — I'm vigorously hetero sexual ha-ha. But of course I don't mean that either. No, no. But anyway. What I discovered was that for some reason people found me — peculiar. Of course I sensed it first from the boys at boarding school. But it was Father with his usual — his usual directness and honesty who made me face it. I remember the day he said to me: 'Had you been born down there' — we were in the library and he pointed down to Ballybeg — 'Had you been born

79

down there, you'd have become the village idiot. Fortunately for you, you were born here and we can absorb you.' Ha-ha. So at nine years of age I knew certain things: that certain kinds of people laughed at me; that the easy relationships that other men enjoy would always elude me; that — that — that I would never succeed in life, whatever — you know — whatever 'succeed' means —

EAMON   Casimir —

CASIMIR No, no, please. That was a very important and a very difficult discovery for me, as you can imagine. But it brought certain recognitions, certain compensatory recognitions. Because once I recognized — once I acknowledged that the larger areas were not accessible to me, I discovered — I had to discover smaller, much smaller areas that were. Yes, indeed. And I discovered that if I conduct myself with some circumspection, I find that I can live within these smaller, perhaps very confined territories without exposure to too much hurt. Indeed I find that I can experience some happiness and perhaps give a measure of happiness, too. My great discovery. Isn't it so beautiful? (*Music*) Somehow the Hall doesn't exist without him. (*He begins pacing again*) We must have a talk sometime, Eamon.

EAMON   Yes.

CASIMIR I don't think we ever had a talk, you and I, had we?

EAMON   I don't think so.

CASIMIR I'd really like to talk to you because I think you — I think you understand — (*he gestures towards the house*) — what it has done to all of us.

EAMON   I don't know about that.

CASIMIR Oh, yes, you do. I know you do. And you would tell me about your work and about London and I would tell you about my boys and about Hamburg. Will you, Eamon, please?

EAMON   Of course.

CASIMIR Good. Great. Next time we meet. We even have our agenda all ready, haven't we? When I went up to see him the evening I arrived — was it only two days ago? — I stood looking down at him and I remembered a poem called 'My Father Dying', and the last lines go:

> But on any one
> of these nights soon
> for you, the dark will not crack with dawn
> And then I will begin
> with you that hesitant conversation
> going on and on and on.

Something disquieting about that line 'going on and on and on', isn't there? Ha-ha.

JUDITH and ALICE enter. CASIMIR resumes pacing. JUDITH in a dark dress and carrying Alice's case. ALICE with coat and handbag. They deposit these things in the study.

ALICE   Thanks. Just leave it there.
JUDITH   When's your bus?
ALICE   We've another fifteen or twenty minutes yet.
JUDITH   Willie'll be here. He said he'll run you down.
ALICE   That'd be handy.

They both come out to the lawn.

There's tea in there if you want it.
EAMON   None for me.
ALICE   Casimir?
CASIMIR   Not at the moment, thank you.
JUDITH   Did you get your flight fixed up?
CASIMIR   Mrs Moore did all the phoning, made all the arrangements. She was wonderful.
JUDITH   Does Helga know?
CASIMIR   I sent her a telegram. I should be home at midnight.

EAMON touches ALICE's cheek with his index finger.

EAMON	It's healed.
ALICE	Is it?
EAMON	Almost.
ALICE	I heal quickly.
EAMON	Sorry.
ALICE	I've packed your things.
EAMON	Thanks.
ALICE	Have you the tickets?

He taps his jacket pocket.

I'll be glad to be home, if it's only to get a sleep. (*Aloud*) Tom hasn't left yet, has he?

JUDITH	He's in the library; some dates he wants to check again.
EAMON	'Check', 'recheck', 'double-check', 'cross-check'.
JUDITH	He's talking about waiting over until the morning.
EAMON	Wasn't he lucky to be here for Father's death. I suppose he'll interpret that as 'the end of an epoch'.
JUDITH	Isn't it?
EAMON	Is it?
CASIMIR	He's from Chicago, he tells me. And I suspect he may be a very wealthy man: his uncle owns the Bell Telephone Company.
EAMON	He should never have been let set foot here.
JUDITH	He asked my permission.
EAMON	To pry?
JUDITH	To chronicle.
EAMON	Ah.
JUDITH	To record the truth.
EAMON	Better still. And you said, 'Go ahead, stranger.'
JUDITH	Is there something to hide?

EAMON *spreads his hands.*

Besides — it's my home.

Brief pause. Then quickly

ALICE	It wasn't exactly the biggest funeral ever seen in Ballybeg, was it?
CASIMIR	Did you notice — the whole village closed down.
ALICE	For the minute it took the hearse to pass through. And as Sister Thérèse would say: 'The multitude in the church was a little empty, too.'
CASIMIR	I thought the Requiem Mass very moving.
ALICE	Until Miss Quirk cut loose. For God's sake did nobody tell her it wasn't the wedding?
JUDITH	She would have played anyway.
ALICE	But maybe not 'This Is My Lovely Day'. Or is that one of the two pieces?
JUDITH	You might have got 'Bless This House'.
ALICE	Father would not have been amused. Casimir, will you please stop prowling around?
CASIMIR	Oh. Sorry — sorry.

He sits — as if he were about to take off again.

ALICE	Who was the man standing just behind Willie at the graveside? — Glasses, pasty-looking, plump, bald. I noticed him in the chapel, too; in the front pew on the men's side.
EAMON	Jerry.
ALICE	Who?
EAMON	Jerry McLaughlin.
ALICE	Who's Jerry Mc — ? Not — !

EAMON *nods.*

For God's sake! But that man could be her father, Judith!

JUDITH	Easy.

The music stops suddenly. Silence.

ALICE	She couldn't have heard me, could she?
CLAIRE	Casimir!
CASIMIR	Hello-hello.

83

CLAIRE   What's the name of this?
ALICE   (*Relieved*) God.

CASIMIR *leaps up.*

CASIMIR   A test! She's testing me again! (*Shouts*) Go ahead! I'm
          ready! I'm waiting!

          *He moves upstage and stands poised, waiting. His
          eyes are shut tight, etc, etc, as before. The music is
          the Ballade in A flat major, Op.47.*

ALICE   You never told me he was like that.
JUDITH   Like what?
ALICE   That's an elderly man. (*To* EAMON) Did you know he
          was like that?
CASIMIR   Good Lord — good Lord — good Lord — good
          Lord —
ALICE   She's only — what? — twenty-seven? Twenty-eight?
CASIMIR   I know it — I know it so well — but what is it? —
          What *is* it? —
ALICE   Thank God the wedding's postponed for three
          months. Maybe she'll come to her senses in the mean-
          time. How could the poor child marry a man like
          that for God's sake?
JUDITH   I've no idea. (*Rises*) There are some things we've got
          to get settled before you all leave. (*Shouts*) Claire,
          could you come out for a few minutes?
ALICE   So that's Jerry McLaughlin.
EAMON   He looks older than he is.
JUDITH   Claire!
ALICE   Oh dear, dear, dear, dear, dear.

          The music stops. CASIMIR *comes downstage.*

CASIMIR   (*To* EAMON) It's a sonata — a sonata — I know that
          — either 58 or 59 — but which? Which?
EAMON   Don't ask me.
ALICE   (*To* EAMON) What age is he?

84

CASIMIR	Oh, Lord, I should know. Alice?
ALICE	What?
CASIMIR	58 or 59?
ALICE	Is he serious?
CASIMIR	59 — that's my guess.
ALICE	He's right.
CASIMIR	Am I?
ALICE	He must be that. Oh, the poor baby!

CLAIRE *enters — she is not wearing mourning clothes.* ALICE *studies her face with anxious compassion.*

CLAIRE	(*To* CASIMIR) Well?
CASIMIR	It's a sonata.
CLAIRE	Is it?
CASIMIR	Isn't it?
ALICE	Claire darling, that was just beautiful playing.
CLAIRE	Thanks.
CASIMIR	Yes; it's a sonata.
CLAIRE	So you've said.
CASIMIR	Is it not?
ALICE	Would you like to sit here, facing the sun?
CLAIRE	I'm fine. (*To* CASIMIR) You don't know!
JUDITH	Please, everybody —
CASIMIR	And it's either — and I'm not absolutely certain —
CLAIRE	You don't know!
JUDITH	Claire —
CASIMIR	It's either the —
JUDITH	May I — ?
CASIMIR	58 — right?
JUDITH	Please may I speak?
CLAIRE	(*Whispers*) Wrong.
CASIMIR	(*Whispers*) 59?
JUDITH	Could I have a moment now that we're all here?
CASIMIR	Sorry — sorry. I beg your pardon, Judith.
CLAIRE	(*Whispers*) Completely wrong.
JUDITH	We haven't got all that much time. (*To* CASIMIR) Here's a seat.

He sits. CLAIRE *grins at him behind Judith's back.*
He signals another answer. She rejects this, too. He
is deflated. ALICE *has not taken her eyes off* CLAIRE.
Now she goes to her.

ALICE I got a glimpse of you coming down the aisle this morning and I had a sudden memory of you coming down on the morning of your First Communion; and you looked exactly the same as you did then — not one day older — a beautiful little innocent child. Hasn't changed a bit, has she? (*She looks round for confirmation; but everyone is silent and waiting*) What's wrong?

JUDITH I would like to talk about what's to happen now that Father's gone — before you all leave.

ALICE Sorry. Sorry. Of course. Go ahead.

JUDITH I know he has left everything to the four of us — the house, the furnishings, the land. And the question is: what are we going to do?

ALICE Well, as far as I'm concerned, my home's in London, Casimir's is in Hamburg, and this house is yours and Claire's. (*To* CASIMIR) Isn't that right?

CASIMIR Oh, yes; oh, yes, indeed.

ALICE Naturally we'll come back now and again. But the Hall must be your home. So the next time we're here we'll sign over to you whatever our share is — or better still have the papers drawn up and sent to us. The important thing is to have it all formal. (*To* CASIMIR) Don't you agree?

CASIMIR I —

ALICE (*To* JUDITH) I see no problem.

EAMON What has Casimir to say?

CASIMIR Me? Oh, yes, Alice is right, absolutely right. I mean I would hope to bring the boys over sometime for a holiday — a short holiday — if I may. But I would be really happy for you to have it all, Judith — and Claire — oh, yes, very happy. You deserve it. It should be yours. It must be yours. Oh, yes.

ALICE So. We're all agreed.

CASIMIR   One small thing: would it be possible — would you mind very much if I took that photo of Mother in the silver frame — a keepsake, you know —

ALICE   That's the one on the drawing-room mantelpiece?

CASIMIR   Yes. It's really very small. But I would — I would really cherish that. If I may.

ALICE   And the sooner the place is in your names the better — before we all have a big row some day! And that's that. All settled. (*To* EAMON) Do we need to keep an eye on the time?

EAMON   Judith has other ideas, I think.

ALICE   Have you? What ideas?

JUDITH   Owning the place, going on living here — it's not as simple as it looks. In fact it's impossible.

ALICE   Why?

JUDITH   We can't afford it. You've forgotten — no, you've never known — the finances of this place. For the past seven years we've lived on Father's pension. That was modest enough. And now that's gone. The only other income is from the land and Willie takes that because no one else would; but that can't continue. So that from now on there's no money coming in. Last October when the storm lifted the whole roof off the back return I tried to get an overdraft from the bank. The manager was very sympathetic but he couldn't help — actually what he said was that the house was a liability.

EAMON   That's bloody —

JUDITH   Then I got a dealer down from Dublin to evaluate the library and some of the furniture. He offered me seventy pounds for the grandmother clock and ninety pounds for the whole library. So eventually Willie and I put up polythene sheets and nailed them to the rafters. And the floor in the morning room has collapsed with dry rot — haven't you seen it? — and every time there's heavy rain, we have to distribute — (*to* CLAIRE) how many is it? — seventeen buckets in the upstairs rooms to catch the water. And the only fire we had all last winter was in Father's bedroom. And on a day like this it looks so beautiful, doesn't it?

Short pause.

ALICE   Judith, God forgive us, we never for a second suspected —
JUDITH   That's just one side of the story.
ALICE   Oh but we can all help. We must. None of us is wealthy but the very least we can do is —
JUDITH   So there's no point in signing the place over to us — well, over to me. I'm not going to go on living here. Maybe Claire —
CLAIRE   I'm getting out, too, amn't I? I'm getting married, amn't I?
ALICE   (*To* JUDITH) Where will you go? What will you do?
JUDITH   The first thing I'm going to do is take the baby out of the orphanage.
ALICE   Of course. Yes.
JUDITH   'The baby' — he's seven now. (*To* CASIMIR) Do you know he's two days younger than your Heinrich? Where I'll go I haven't made up my mind yet. Willie has a mobile home just outside Bundoran. He has a lot of slot-machines around that area and he wants me to go there with him.
ALICE   That would be —
JUDITH   But he doesn't want the baby. So that settles that. Anyhow I've got to earn a living somehow. But the only reason I brought all this up is — what's to become of Uncle George?
EAMON   What you're saying is that after Claire's wedding — if you can wait that length — you're going to turn the key in the door and abandon Ballybeg Hall?
JUDITH   I'm asking —
EAMON   You know what will happen, don't you? The moment you've left the thugs from the village will move in and loot and ravage the place within a couple of hours. Is that what you're proposing? Oh, your piety is admirable.

JUDITH   I'm asking what's to become of Uncle George.

EAMON   Judith's like her American friend: the Hall can be assessed in terms of roofs and floors and overdrafts.

ALICE   Eamon —

EAMON   No, no; that's all it means to her. Well I know its real worth — in this area, in this county, in this country. And Alice knows. And Casimir knows. And Claire knows. And somehow we'll keep it going. Somehow we'll keep it going. Somehow we'll —

ALICE   Please, Eamon.

JUDITH *breaks down. Pause.*

EAMON   Sorry — sorry — sorry again — Seems to be a day of public contrition. What the hell is it but crumbling masonry. Sorry. (*Short laugh*) Don't you know that all that is fawning and forelock-touching and Paddy and shabby and greasy peasant in the Irish character finds a house like this irresistible? That's why we were ideal for colonizing. Something in us needs this — aspiration. Don't despise us — we're only hedge-hogs, Judith. Sorry.

He goes to the gazebo.

ALICE   He hates going back to London. He hates the job. (*Pause*) What is there to say? There's nothing to say, is there?

JUDITH   No.

Silence. CLAIRE *rises and crosses the lawn. As she passes* CASIMIR

CLAIRE   A ballade.

CASIMIR   Sorry?

CLAIRE   Ballade A flat major.

CASIMIR   (*Indifferently*) Ah. Was it really? No, I'd never have got that. There you are. Never.

He gets up and begins his pacing. Pause.

ALICE   So the baby's seven now?

JUDITH   Eight next month.

ALICE   The woman in the flat above us has a little girl. She comes in to us every evening after school. Eamon buys her sweets. She's devoted to him. He's great with children.

JUDITH   Yes?

ALICE   Avril. Avril Harper. Lovely affectionate child.

JUDITH   What age is she?

ALICE   She's just eight.

JUDITH   They say that's a very interesting age.

ALICE   She's a very interesting child. And a very affectionate child.

The conversation dies again. ALICE *rises.*

CASIMIR   (*To* CLAIRE) There's still some clay on your shoes.

CLAIRE   Did you notice a wreath of red and yellow roses at the foot of the grave? That was from the children I taught last winter. There were five of them and they put their pocket money together to buy it. Wasn't that kind of them? And each of them came up to me in turn and shook my hand very formally and said how sorry they were. I asked them to be sure and visit me in my new home. They said they would. I made them promise. They said they would.

Another silence.

ALICE   Are you sure Willie's coming?

JUDITH   Yes; he knows; he'll be here.

ALICE   Time enough anyway.

CASIMIR   There was a telegram from the Bishop, Judith.

JUDITH   Yes.

CASIMIR   Out on the hall table.

JUDITH   I saw it.

ALICE   What did it say?

CASIMIR Deepest sympathy to you all and to George on your
         great loss — something like that.
JUDITH   We still haven't reached a decision about Uncle
         George.

         CASIMIR *suddenly stops pacing and exclaims —
         almost wails — in his panic.*

CASIMIR Oh my God!
CLAIRE   What?
CASIMIR Oh good God!

         *He dashes into the study, as always tripping on the
         step and apologising over his shoulder.*

         Sorry — sorry — I beg your —

         *He rushes to the phone. His sudden departure
         shatters the mood.* EAMON *comes out of the gazebo.
         The others come together.*

ALICE   What's wrong, Casimir?
EAMON   What happened?
JUDITH   Is he ill?
ALICE   I don't know. He suddenly bolted.
CLAIRE   Listen!
EAMON   Is he sick?
CLAIRE   Listen!
CASIMIR Hello? Hello? Yes, Mrs Moore, it's me again. I'm
         afraid. I'm a nuisance, amn't I? That telegram I sent
         to Germany — Yes, yes, indeed the house will be
         lonely — Very nice sermon, indeed; very moving —
         I'll tell her that; of course I will; thank you very
         much —
ALICE   I thought he was going to be sick.
CASIMIR That telegram I sent to Germany an hour ago, Mrs
         Moore — has it gone? Ah. Well. That's that — No,
         no, I'm not complaining — oh, no — I'm delighted,
         thank you, absolutely delighted, thank you —

He rings off and comes outside. He is thoroughly
wretched. Everybody is staring at him. He man-
ages one of his grins.

CASIMIR   Ha-ha. Oh good God.

ALICE   Is something wrong?

CLAIRE   What's the matter, Casimir?

CASIMIR   Sent a telegram to Helga. To let her know I'd be home tonight.

ALICE   And so you will.

CASIMIR   Yes.

JUDITH   What's wrong, Casimir?

CASIMIR   Tried to cancel it but it's gone. I told you she's a great believer in that spiritualist stuff — seances, ghosts, things — I told you that, didn't I? Yes, I did. Well, you see, I've only suddenly realized what I said in the telegram. What I said was — FATHER BURIED THIS MORNING ARRIVING HAMBURG MIDNIGHT TONIGHT. Ha-ha. Oh my God.

> *Their sympathy for his genuine anguish prevents*
> *them from laughing outright. But* CLAIRE *sniggers*
> *first — then* ALICE *— then they all collapse. And*
> *finally he joins them. Comments like 'Arriving*
> *Hamburg midnight tonight', 'I thought he was*
> *sick', 'He said "I'm absolutely delighted, Mrs*
> *Moore"', 'Poor Father in Germany'. In the middle of*
> *this release* UNCLE GEORGE *enters right in his usual*
> *manner.* ALICE *sees him first. She looks at him —*
> *then makes a sudden decision. She rushes to* EAMON.

ALICE   Do me a favour, Eamon.

EAMON   What?

ALICE   A big favour — please?

EAMON   What is it?

ALICE   Uncle George — let us take him.

EAMON   To London?

ALICE   Please, Eamon.

EAMON   He wouldn't come.

ALICE   Let me try. Please.

EAMON   Would he come?

ALICE   (*Calls*) Uncle George!

> *He stops just as he is about to make his retreat. She goes to him.*

I want you to come to London with Eamon and me. You wouldn't have to talk. You wouldn't ever have to say a word. But you'd be great company for me, just being there. I wouldn't be lonely if you were there with me.

> ALICE *reaches forward to catch his hand but withdraws again. Long pause. Then —*

GEORGE   Haven't been in London since the year nineteen and ten; to be precise the week Edward the Seventh died. Saw it all. That's what *I* call a funeral.

ALICE   Will you come? Please.

> *Short pause.*

GEORGE   Another visit's about due, I suppose. I'll pack.

> *He marches off the way he came.*

ALICE   Thank you, Uncle George — thank you. (*Elated, to* EAMON) He's coming! (*To all*) He's coming with us to London! Do you mind?

EAMON   Where will he sleep?

ALICE   On the divan — anywhere — he won't mind — he never cared about his comfort. You're sure you don't mind?

EAMON   He'll be *my* keepsake.

> WILLIE *enters through the study.*

WILLIE   Sorry I'm a bit late. Who needs a lift down to the bus?

93

ALICE	Thanks, Willie. I suppose we should start moving.
CASIMIR	Time enough yet, aren't we?
JUDITH	Anybody feel like something to eat?
WILLIE	No time for eating now.
JUDITH	(*To* EAMON) A cup of tea?
EAMON	No thanks.
JUDITH	A drink?
EAMON	Nothing.
ALICE	How long a delay have you in London before your Hamburg flight?
CASIMIR	An hour and a half.
ALICE	We'll stay with you at the airport and eat there.
JUDITH	(*To* WILLIE) Uncle George is going with Alice and Eamon.
WILLIE	Going where?
JUDITH	London.
WILLIE	You're joking me. Are you serious?
JUDITH	Yes.
WILLIE	Jaysus, he'll fair keep London in chat.

They are all seated again: CLAIRE *close to* CASIMIR; WILLIE *beside* JUDITH; EAMON *on the ground at* ALICE's *feet, his head resting against her leg; the three couples spread across the lawn. There is an unspoken wish to protract time, to postpone the final breaking up.* CASIMIR *picks up the cassette.*

CASIMIR	What'll it be?
CLAIRE	Your pleasure.
CASIMIR	My pleasure — right.
CLAIRE	But not a test.
CASIMIR	Not a test; no more tests; just my pleasure.

Pause.

WILLIE	They gave him a nice enough wee send off, didn't they?
JUDITH	Yes.
WILLIE	I was up in court before him once — did I ever tell

94

	you that one?
JUDITH	What was that?
WILLIE	First car I ever had. No tax, no insurance, no licence, no brakes, no nothing — buck all except that the damn thing kind of went. Jaysus. And I mind I swore a pack of lies to him.
JUDITH	Were you fined?
WILLIE	Let me off with a caution! He must have believed me. No, he didn't. Knew damn well I was a liar. He just pretended he believed me. Jaysus, he was a strange bird. How are you?
JUDITH	Slight headache. It's nothing.
WILLIE	I thought so — I was watching you in the chapel. Here.
JUDITH	What's that?
WILLIE	Aspirin. Got them on the way up.
JUDITH	Thanks. I'll take them later.

Bedtime Waltz on the cassette.

| WILLIE | I don't want to hustle yous; but if you're getting the 3.30 you'd need to start moving. |

Nobody hears him.

CASIMIR	You're too young to remember Mother singing that.
CLAIRE	Am I?
CASIMIR	Oh, yes; much too young.
CLAIRE	I think I remember her — I'm not sure. You'll come back again for my wedding, won't you?
CASIMIR	Wouldn't miss it for all the world. Three months time, isn't it?
CLAIRE	I wish it were tomorrow. I would love it would be tomorrow.
CASIMIR	Three months? Oh my goodness three months'll fly — just fly. We'll all be back again before you know. What's three months? Three months is nothing, nothing, nothing.

Brief pause.

ALICE   What are you thinking?

EAMON   That in a way it's as difficult for me as it is for you.

ALICE   What is?

EAMON   Leaving; leaving for good. I know it's your home. But in a sense it has always been my home, too, because of Granny and then because of you.

ALICE   I don't know what I feel. Maybe a sense of release; of not being pursued; of the possibility of — (*short pause*) — of 'fulfilment'. No. Just emptiness. Perhaps maybe a new start. Yes, I'll manage.

EAMON   Because you're of that tradition.

ALICE   What tradition?

EAMON   Of discipline; of self-discipline — residual aristocratic instincts.

ALICE   I'm the alcoholic, remember.

EAMON   So was Uncle George — once.

ALICE   You and Judith always fight.

EAMON   No, we don't. When did you discover that?

ALICE   I've always known it. And I think it's because you love her. I think it's because you think you love her; and that's the same thing. No, it's even more disturbing for you. And that's why I'm not unhappy that this is all over — because love is possible only in certain contexts. And now that this is finished, you may become less unhappy in time.

EAMON   Have we a context?

ALICE   Let's wait and see.

WILLIE   Does nobody want to catch this bus?

JUDITH   Don't worry, Willie. They'll make it.

> CASIMIR *has been humming with the cassette. Now he stops.*

CASIMIR What you must all do — what you must all do very soon — is come to Hamburg for a holiday! Helga and I have some wonderful friends you'll enjoy meeting — novelists, poets, painters, musicians! —

96

	marvellous people! — and we'll have a great re-union of the whole family! It will be like old times! Everybody'll come next summer! Next summer in Hamburg!
EAMON	A party in Vienna.
CASIMIR	Yes, yes, yes indeed, Eamon! Exactly! That's what it'll be — a party in Vienna!

CLAIRE switches off the cassette player.

CLAIRE	(*Calmly*) I'm suddenly sick of Chopin — isn't that strange? Just suddenly sick of him. I don't think I'll ever play Chopin again.

Silence. Then EAMON begins to sing softly.

EAMON	'Oh don't you remember Sweet Alice, Ben Bolt — '
WILLIE	I'm telling you, Eamon, that aul' bus isn't going to wait for you, you know.
ALICE	'Sweet Alice with hair so brown — '

EAMON and ALICE sing together.

'She wept with delight when you gave her a smile
And trembled with fear at your frown — '

While they are singing the line above

JUDITH	I keep thinking I hear sounds from that speaker.

WILLIE begins to rise.

WILLIE	I'll take it down now.
JUDITH	Don't touch it! (*Softer*) Not just now. Not just at this moment.

CASIMIR has walked round to EAMON and ALICE and sings with them. All three

'In the old church yard in the valley, Ben Bolt
In a corner obscure and alone
They have fitted a slab of granite so grey
And Sweet Alice lies under the stone — '

> *While they are singing,* UNCLE GEORGE *has
> entered the study. He puts his small case on the
> ground and his coat across a chair and sits with his
> hands on his lap. He has all the patience in the
> world.*
>
> *As he sings* CASIMIR *glances over the house.*
> CLAIRE *begins to hum. One has the impression that
> this afternoon — easy, relaxed, relaxing — may go
> on indefinitely.*

WILLIE I'm telling you — they're going to miss it!
JUDITH No, they won't.
WILLIE They're cutting it close then. Jaysus they're cutting it
        very close.
SINGERS 'They have fitted a slab of granite so grey
         And Sweet Alice lies under the stone — '

> *Before the song ends bring the lights down slowly
> to dark.*